THE INTRIGUING WORLD OF
CHINESE HOME COOKING

Cooking Secrets from the Kitchen of
Angela Chang

譚彥 著

海外家常菜

Published by

Life Style Cultural & Media Enterprise Co., Ltd.
10nd Fl. No.77. Lane700.
Chung Chen Road,
Hsin Tien City, Taipei, Taiwan
R. O. C.
Phone: (02) 8218-2757
Fax :   (02) 8218-2685
ISBN   957-0497-37-8

Distributed by

General Agent in North America : J & H Books
J & H Books
6300 Wilshire Blvd., Suite 130
LA.CA. 90048 U.S.A
Tel : 323-4971089

For my parents,

whose love immensely enriched my life.

Contents

ACKNOWLEDGMENT

This book is the result of many years of research and preparation and generous help from many wonderful friends.

First and foremost, I must give my most sincere thanks to Mr. George Kwei, at Human Culture Publishing Company in Taiwan, for his enthusiastic response to my manuscript and his efficient arrangements for the production of color photographs for this book. His confidence and support energized me tremendously as I was attempting to upgrade this book.

I am deeply grateful to the schools that offered me scholarships to study the English language — Providence University in Taiwan and Ball State University in Indiana. Their financial assistance and academic programs more than three decades ago made it possible for me to carry out my dream — writing in my second language.

I am forever indebted to my deceased mother and to the late Rev. Raymond de Jaegher for giving me the encouragement and support that enabled me to pursue my life goals.

I must give special credit to a wonderful host family — Mr. and Mrs. Martin Schwartz in Muncie, Indiana — for their kindness and generosity when I first came to America. It was this hospitable couple who discovered my cooking talent and gave me the most crucial early encouragement.

Gratitude is due to a group of very supportive friends — Faith Bahadurian, Fiona Hinton, Mea Kaemmerlen, Beverly Leach and Tillie Helms for editing and proofreading this book. Special thanks are offered to Isabel Liang, Lucia Hu, Jean Proccacino and Barbara Walsh for testing my recipes, and to Philip Liang for his technical support.

I am extremely honored to acknowledge my mentor, Melanie Barnard, the well-known cookbook author. She has guided me through some difficult times during the course of publishing this book.

Credit is also extended to the talented cooks in the family and among my church friends — especially my sisters-in-law and mother-in-law — whose rich cooking knowledge has inspired me in so many ways and helped to shape my own culinary style.

My sweet and loyal friend, Jane Wan, deserves my heartfelt gratitude for her arduous assistance during the production of this book. Thanks must also go to my colleagues at the Culinary Society of Philadelphia: To Joe Colanero and Irene Rothschild for their expert advice and inspiration; to Margaret Kuo and Ava Hirsh for their encouragement and support; and to many others for sharing my foods and giving me invaluable insights.

During the long period of producing this book, I lost two very dear friends — Dorothy Coot and Sally Chen, both of whom made valuable contributions to the progress of this book. Dottie edited my first draft with true devotion, Sally gave me her most generous friendship and earnest support throughout this cookbook project, Both deserve special credit and loving mention.

This acknowledgment would not be complete without mentioning Michael Wu, President of Wan Ja Shan Soy Sauce Co., who has contributed to my cookbook projects in significant ways.

Last, but not least, my hugs and thanks go to my beloved husband, Humphrey, for his patience and continuous support of this project and to my son Raymond, for teaching me to use the computer.

INTRODUCTION

Cooking has fascinated me since my childhood in Taiwan and I attribute this to my mother's influence. My mother was an extremely hospitable woman who had passion for friends and entertaining. During the month of the Chinese New Year celebration, she would put all the women in the house to work and turn the kitchen into a kind of temporary "food factory." The scene that continues to touch me in my dreams is of my parents' old house, packed with visitors, and of the aroma of delectable foods that permeated throughout. As a young child, I was greatly impressed by the skills of those home cooks. It always amazed me how a few pieces of tofu and fish could be turned into a tasty dish and how plain flour dough could be molded into beautiful-looking dumplings. I never dreamed that one day I could do all this with confidence and that I would go on to teach others about the secrets of Chinese home cooking.

As the youngest daughter in a traditional Chinese household, I had no need to be near the kitchen. Yet, being a curious and adventurous person, I had always had the urge to reproduce the dishes that had intrigued me. The time came after my high school graduation when I had to work away from home and needed to cook my own meals to save money. With my meager salary and limited knowledge of cooking, I was quite happy with what I could turn out. This trivial hobby (which was what people thought about cooking in those days) soon came to an end when I started preparing myself for higher education.

It was not until a few years later when I left my country and went to Indiana to start my graduate studies that I started cooking Chinese food again, partly for survival and partly for entertaining. Winters in Muncie were bitter cold and studies were difficult at times, but the memories of cooking for friends and my host family are always sweet and warm. Whatever I cooked in my limited way was invariably received with love and genuine appreciation.

My real adventure in cooking, however, began soon after my marriage in 1969. At first, cooking was more of a necessity than a hobby. I gradually found out that my husband, Humphrey, has an extremely critical palate. He likes finely cut, light and well-flavored food. To meet his standards, I needed to use more care and creativity in cooking than I ordinarily did for myself.

Another reason for upgrading my cooking skills came from my desire to entertain visiting relatives and friends. I feel almost like my late mother when I pour my heart and energy into providing the best food that I could to delight my guests. And the more involved I have become with cooking, the more rewarding I have found it. To me, cooking is almost therapeutic because no other endeavor brings me such immediate satisfaction. Another lure of cooking for me is that through sharing my foods I have met some truly wonderful friends who have made positive changes in my life. Friendship aside, they have helped me to polish my cooking skills, enabling me to expand my horizons from Chinese cooking to Western baking and eventually to writing cookbooks.

Other than sharing my happy experiences in cooking, the purpose of writing this book is to explore the fascinating world of Chinese home cooking beyond stereotypical Chinese restaurant food. Indeed, the time has come for Chinese cuisine to shed its image of a cheap ethnic food and to move to a higher status. Years ago, people ate Chinese food for its soothing wonton soup, aromatic egg rolls and fried rice. Nowadays, Westerners enjoy Chinese cooking for its marvelous variety of regional flavors and sophisticated ways of handling ingredients. In addition, health conscious cooks in this country are discovering a whole spectrum of intriguing vegetarian products, which are high in flavor but low in calories, at Chinese markets. For these reasons, Chinese cooking has become part of America's mainstream food.

However, despite an array of Chinese ingredients displayed on the supermarket shelves, the puzzling question of how to properly use these newly added foodstuffs remain unanswered. While you may or may not find help from other sources, you will be delighted to discover that this book offers up-to-date food knowledge that will make your cooking experiments not only interesting, but will also help

you enjoy the economical and convenient aspects of Chinese cooking. You will find tips on handling every category of food (including tofu, vegetables, meats, noodles and rice) and also learn to use the major condiments correctly and efficiently. By following the guidelines in this book, you will find shopping at Chinese markets or dining at dim sum houses more interesting and pleasurable. Furthermore, from the histories and stories of Chinese food in this book, you will learn to appreciate this cuisine with a new perspective.

My criteria for selecting recipes include ease of preparation, uniqueness, healthfulness, eye-appeal, convenience and economy. I did not present recipes by region in this book since most home cooks, especially those who grew up in Taiwan, embrace all regional tastes. The reason Cantonese cuisine and Sichuan cuisine are repeatedly mentioned is that these two regions have had the most profound influence on Chinese home cooking. Friends who tested my recipes have found that many dishes can be made ahead of time and served cold, which easily fits into

the schedule of working mothers and are ideal for home entertaining.

The fact that most Chinese are not overweight is proof that the Chinese diet is light and healthy. We use rice or noodles as a filling staple, accompanied by a great variety of vegetarian products (including greens, root vegetables, beans and tofu) cooked alone or with a small amount of meat. We emphasize the balance of taste and texture in a meal (which simultaneously includes the major food groups) rather than excluding meat from our diet completely. I believe that a vast range of vegetarian products, superb sauces and efficient cooking methods are what make Chinese dishes so tasty and satisfying that we have almost no snacking needs (a drink or sweets here and there can add up to a lot of calories and fats).

The important thing about cooking Chinese dishes is not so much about cutting down on oil totally, but to use it with good judgment. You do need a couple of tablespoons of oil to sizzle the aromatics for a big plate of food. However, if you feel uneasy using more than 1 tablespoonful, then, by all means, adjust the amount according to your own needs. Using a non-stick pan or wok will also help you to cut down on the amount of oil in your stir-fried dishes.

I have repeatedly told my students that, in certain aspects, cooking Chinese dishes is like cooking Western dishes. You need a thorough understanding of the ingredients and the basic techniques before you embark on your adventures. I have seen novices who failed in their attempts at Chinese cooking because they had selected the wrong ingredients or used them improperly. For example, some people have the notion that five-spice powder and sesame oil enhance the flavors of all kinds of dishes, so they use them lavishly on everything. I have also seen a local chef who used sesame oil indiscriminately in all stir-fried dishes. This is a mistake. Since these condiments are very strong by nature, they should be used sparingly whenever they are called for. I must stress that sesame oil is seasoning oil, not cooking oil.

Tofu, cellophane noodles, sticky rice and taro root have received special attention in this book. The potential of these ingredients is still waiting to be explored. You don't have to use them only in Chinese cooking; they are wonderful by themselves. Simply playing with these novelties can be great fun.

Another advantage of cooking Chinese dishes is that you don't have to use exact measurements for everything. For example, a slight difference in the amount of cooking wine, vinegar, sugar or aromatics will not drastically affect results at all. The trick is to first start with a small amount, then constantly taste and adjust your mixture to ensure a balanced flavor. With the cooking knowledge you learn from this book and with a little care, you are on your way to a new culinary adventure.

A unique part of this book is the chapter on Chinese sweets, "Reinventing Chinese Sweets." While many food authorities perceive traditional Chinese cakes and desserts as uninteresting, I believe they are a lost art and I have been persistent in finding the real stories behind them. The opportunity came when I had to stay in Taiwan for five months to produce pictures for this book. During my visits to several major cities, I had the good fortune of meeting the most skillful chefs in the country. Interviews with these chefs helped me collect valuable information on Chinese pastries for my readers. I hope this chapter will spark some interest among gourmets.

I would like to comment on the photos in this book. I must admit that it was rather risky for me to accept a complicated cooking assignment during the hot summer months in Taiwan. At the beginning, a shower a day was like mercy from heaven, which made the weather more bearable. But by mid-July, with temperature soaring to 100 degrees, it was extremely difficult working in a kitchen with only one fan blowing hot air. Trying to speed up my job in order to escape the heat, I found it impossible to keep track of how each dish should look. Thus, inevitably, small differences between a few recipes and their pictures could occur — in the ways ingredients are cut and dishes are garnished, or in the amount of sauces used. As such, I hope my readers will use the pictures only as a guide — let your judgment and creativity lead you into a world of exciting and satisfying culinary adventures.

A NOTE ABOUT CHINESE SPICES AND SEASONINGS

The Art of Flavoring

Confucius once said: "I will not eat anything that is not seasoned with good sauce." This seems to have spelled out the key ingredient of good cooking — flavoring. Indeed, a well-cooked dish should not lack the subtle taste that truly delights the palate—"deeply penetrated flavor," as the Chinese call it. However, to achieve this goal is no easy task for the unskilled cook. This is the reason why mastering the art of flavoring is such a sought-after skill.

Backed by centuries of culinary history, Chinese cuisine is blessed with a multitude of cooking methods and an astonishingly wide range of seasoning ingredients that make Chinese cooking more than just palatable. As you explore it, you'll find it intriguing, extraordinary and sometimes full of happy surprises.

In Chinese cuisine, as in Western cuisine, herbs and spices are used extensively in sauces, but Chinese sauces are more complex in make-up and their tastes more subtle. Many Western cooks think that using bamboo leaves, lotus leaves and dried vegetables in the seasoning of foods is quite an unusual technique, and therefore, worth exploring. Perhaps they will be even more impressed when they learn that the Chinese also rely on dried seafood (such as dried shrimp or dried fish) to enhance the flavor of many popular home dishes.

Regional Cuisines

And here is the key ingredient that plays a large part in differentiating the regional tastes in Chinese cuisine — the use of certain special seasonings.

Northern Cuisine (Beijing and Shandong) is known for its rich elegant banquet dishes and its delectable dumplings and noodles. The dominant seasonings are bean sauces (especially sweet bean sauce), garlic and scallions.

Eastern Cuisine (Shanghai and Suzhou) is known for the elaborate "red-cooked" dishes, the cold cut meats and the sophisticated snacks and pastries. In this area, dark soy sauce, rock sugar and five-spice powder are used extensively.

Cantonese Cuisine is reputed for its broad spectrum in seafood casseroles, the mild but flavorful stir-fried dishes and dim sum snacks. Favorite sauces include oyster sauce, black bean sauce and Sha Cha sauce (originally from Malaysia).

Sichuan and Hunan Cuisines are growing in popularity. Two of the region's most famous and pungent ingredients — Sichuan peppercorns and pickled mustard green — have found their way into every Chinese kitchen. Their unique and distinctive properties fascinate even Western gourmets. Sichuan dishes are rich but not heavy, robust but not overpowering. Lingering, subtle taste is perhaps their secret ingredient.

In modern Chinese kitchens, home cooking is not restricted to dishes from the family's hometown but embraces other regional flavors as well. Modern Chinese home cooks use any spices and herbs that can easily transform their foods into a tasty meal. For newcomers, however, I heartily suggest that you have a thorough understanding of the properties and characteristics of major Chinese seasoning ingredients before you start using them.

Types of Seasonings

One characteristic of Chinese cooking that distinguishes it from Western cuisine is the seasoning, which is invariably done before or during the course of cooking. At its final stage, each dish is expected to meet certain criteria regarding aroma, flavor and color. If any additional flavoring were needed at all, it would probably be a dash of black pepper or a touch of aromatics. To shower salt or soy sauce on freshly cooked Chinese food without first tasting it can ruin the good flavor of the dish.

A detailed description of seasoning ingredients can be found in the Glossary of Ingredients (page 204). To give you a better understanding of seasonings and the role they play in Chinese cuisine, I have divided them into the following groups according to their general functions:

Basic Seasonings: Oil, salt, pepper, vinegar, cooking wine, soy sauce, sugar, sesame oil and cornstarch. These are the fundamental ingredients used commonly in marinades to flavor or tenderize meats, or added during cooking to give flavor to the dish. Sometimes they are added at the end of cooking or just before serving to give extra zest to the dish. They are also served simply as dipping sauces.

Sauces: Oyster sauce, fermented black beans, chili bean sauce, yellow bean sauce, sha cha sauce, wine sauce, mixed sauces (such as sweet and sour sauce), Sichuan sauce and Hunan sauce. These are enrichment sauces used mainly to accentuate flavors and are usually added during cooking.

Spices: Sichuan peppercorns, star anise, cinnamon sticks, five-spice powder, chili powder, curry powder and orange peels. These are often used in stews, red-cooked dishes and occasionally in stir-fried dishes.

Aromatics
Ginger, garlic, scallions, cilantro and Chinese chives. These play a vital part in Chinese cooking. They are used widely in marinating, stir-frying, garnishing, Chinese-style salad dressing and dipping sauces.

Dried Foods as Seasonings: Dried scallops, dried fish, dried shrimp, dried squid, dried mushrooms, dried cabbage and cured meats. This group marks the sophistication of Chinese seasoning. Dried foods have a richer concentrated flavor than their fresh forms. All of these unique products require soaking to reconstitute to the "live" stages. They are excellent flavor enhancers for soups, or stir-fried and steamed dishes.

Marinating

Chinese meat dishes are always tender and flavorful when brought to the table and this is due to a very important step—marinating. Marinating serves two purposes: first, it eliminates or masks the gamy odor of meats and the fishy smell of fish, giving them a basic flavor; second, it tenderizes meats by forming a protective coat to seal in the juices and flavors during cooking. But a marinade is hardly strong enough to permeate the whole dish if the meat is cooked with other ingredients. This is when additional flavoring sauce is required during or toward the end of cooking.

Adjusting To Taste

Many experienced Chinese home cooks never use a

measuring spoon during cooking. Instead, they judge the amount used partly by experience and partly by repeated tasting. Here is my suggestion: whether you are an experienced cook or a novice, it is always safer to taste your food before removing it from the wok. No matter how closely you follow the recipe, there is always a chance that it might not turn out to your liking. Should this happen, there are several ways you can improve upon it. If the flavor is too light, try adding a little soy sauce or oyster sauce. If it is too flat, try a teaspoon of sugar (or stock), sesame oil or vinegar. Adding a small amount of good chili bean sauce will also spice up a bland dish.

Choosing Sauces

The ability to use sauces properly is a crucial step in Chinese cooking. This is what makes cooking Chinese dishes such an interesting and enjoyable activity. However, many Western cooks find it difficult to choose from the wide variety of sauces displayed in Chinese markets. What you should buy depends on whether you are a conservative cook or an adventurous cook. If you want to keep it simple by sticking to one sauce, then your safest bet would be a bottle of oyster sauce. In many cases, 1 or 2 teaspoonfuls of oyster sauce accompanied by a few tablespoonfuls of chicken broth is often enough to flavor your dishes. But if you like to exercise your taste buds with the excitement of various exotic sauces, then, by all means, try these popular Chinese condiments: fermented black beans, sweet bean sauce, chili paste, sha cha sauce and Sichuan peppercorns.

Blending Sauces

Seasoning sauces which are used in marinades, stir-fried dishes and dipping sauces are often made by combining several ingredients to give the food an intense flavor. Not every dish needs a mixed sauce. Those with natural good flavor require only a light touch of salt, pepper, or soy sauce and sesame oil. But bland dishes and meats with pronounced strong taste can be improved with a heavily mixed sauce that will add or mask flavors. In reading through Chinese recipes, you will find many ways of combining sauces. One effective way is to mix aromatics — ginger, garlic, scallions, or cilantro — with basic sauces such as soy sauce, sesame oil or oyster sauce. You can make a small jar of master sauce and use it for all your Chinese dishes. A word about dipping sauces: Since all Chinese dishes are well flavored, additional seasonings are absolutely unnecessary. The only time a dipping sauce is called for is when serving dumplings, unseasoned fried foods, certain cold cuts and fire pots.

MSG

When discussing Chinese seasonings, many readers are inclined to ask a very controversial question: "Is MSG really bad for you?" Personally, I have never used MSG in my cooking. I believe that with a good stock and some good sauces on hand, a confident cook can live well without MSG. Some restaurants depend on MSG perhaps because it is harder to flavor large quantities of food. But if you think that MSG is a Chinese specialty, you are wrong; this seasoning is widely used in most of your favorite foods such as potato chips, tortillas, canned goods and sausages. MSG is actually a vegetable by-product that is harmless to most people; but for a small number of diners, MSG can cause severe reactions. When cooking for others, it is best not to use it.

TIPS AND TECHNIQUES

Stir-Frying

In the last few decades, this cooking method, which is perhaps the best known of all Chinese cooking techniques, has caught the attention of cooks in American kitchens. This is justifiable because stir-frying has many attractive features.

To begin with, it is quick and economical. Moreover, it is also an efficient way of cooking that retains the natural flavor of foods by preserving the texture, color and nutrients of the ingredients. During stir-frying, intense heat and hot oil add a new dimension of taste to food by coating it with a special aroma. This is the reason why meat and vegetables are first stir-fried separately and then combined to blend the flavors. Stir-frying the ingredients separately gives them a chance to be touched by the "wok heat" (a term used by the Cantonese when referring to the intense heat from the wok). In other words, stir-frying is like sautéing, but performed on a larger scale.

For successful stir-frying, remember these helpful guidelines:

Preparation

Thorough preparation is essential. This includes selecting the freshest ingredients obtainable, as the quality of the raw materials significantly affects the taste of the dish. During preparation, different ingredients are handled separately. First, the meat must be cut into the proper size and marinated briefly to give it a basic flavor. Adding a little oil to the meat before stir-frying can prevent it from toughening and sticking together.

Vegetables must be picked and trimmed carefully. The Chinese are very finicky about this, so the tough parts, the blemished sections and the strings should all be removed. When preparing leafy vegetables, it is critical to rinse out the grit and shake off as much water as possible since excess water can cause the temperature to drop drastically, thus affecting the taste of the dish. And to avoid last minute confusion (especially for novices), it is advisable to have all dried and liquid ingredients ready before you actually start cooking.

Temperature Control

Temperature control is crucial to successful stir-frying. Although stir-frying generally requires intense heat and hot oil, we should use our judgment to vary the intensity of the heat according to the size and texture of the ingredients.

As a rule, all vegetables require the highest flame possible for the best result (especially vegetables with a high water content, such as bean sprouts, cucumbers and cabbage). For leafy vegetables, stems have to be cooked about one minute longer than leaves; therefore, you should always separate them and add the stems to the hot oil first. They should be tossed quickly and cooked within 2 to 3 minutes so that the natural flavor and color of the ingredients are retained.

However, temperature control for meat is slightly different. Large pieces and chunks require a fierce flame to brown nicely. For small pieces like strips and thin slices, use a medium flame at the start to break them apart; then increase the heat to high in order to heat and brown them properly. Delicate meats like chicken breast, baby shrimp and scallops should be treated with special care. They need to be stirred over a medium-high flame just until the rawness disappears or they will lose the tender texture so valued by gourmets.

Steaming

Steaming is a versatile cooking technique that is used extensively in Chinese kitchens, whereas in Western kitchens it is not a frequently used cooking technique. In ancient China, ovens were found mainly in commercial kitchens and they were used primarily for roasting meats.

The modern oven is a recent addition to Chinese restaurants and home kitchens. The lack of this useful appliance in the past has not deterred Chinese cooks from making baked confectioneries like dough, cakes and pastries. Chinese cooks improvised by steaming the confectioneries instead of baking them.

To the Chinese, the purpose of steaming is threefold: First, to keep the natural and "pure" taste of the ingredients, as in steamed fish. Second, to preserve the original appearance of the foods, as in dumpling dishes. Third, to minimize the greasy taste of certain high-fat dishes such as Spiced Bacon.

To achieve the best results in steaming, follow these rules:

Freshness

Since the steamed dish reveals the true taste of the ingredients, it is paramount that the raw materials are at the peak of their freshness. If this is not the case, then it is better to cook them by sautéing or deep-frying.

Marinating

The ingredients must be thoroughly marinated (at least 15 minutes) before being steamed. The recommended seasonings for steamed fish or meats are wine, soy sauce (or salt), ginger, scallions, chili bean sauce, Sichuan peppercorns and black beans. For steaming vegetables Chinese-style, you must first stir-fry and fully flavor them before steaming.

Temperature Control

Always wait until the water comes to a boil before putting the ingredients in the steamer. To prevent the heat from escaping, avoid checking too frequently.

When more water is needed during steaming, be sure to use hot water. This will maintain the high temperature.

Vary the heat and the steaming time according to the type of ingredients used. The rule of thumb is to use high heat and short steaming time for tender ingredients such as fish or stir-fried vegetables, which need little cooking; and medium heat and longer steaming time for hard ingredients such as chunks of meat, which require long steaming.

Deep-Frying

Deep-frying can do an excellent job in the following areas:
* To mask any unpleasant taste of the ingredients.
* To accentuate the flavors of seasoned meats, fish and other foodstuffs.
* To give a crispy texture and new taste to foods.

Deep-frying has a more prominent place in Chinese restaurant cooking (also in banquet dishes) than in home cooking. Many great dishes rely on this important step for their golden color, crispy skin and aroma.

It is ironic that although Chinese home cooking abounds in deep-fried dishes, fried foods are not commonly served at home, perhaps because they are time-consuming, fattening and messy. Nevertheless, fried foods are too tempting to be left out entirely.

Ingredients for deep-frying should be treated the same way as they are in other forms of cooking—they should be cut uniformly then marinated. Again, temperature control is the crucial factor in deep-frying. Here are the rules of thumb for successful deep-frying:

Temperature Control
Aim for the right temperature. It should never be too high or too low. The oil should be hot when adding foods to it. To check the temperature of the oil, drop a small piece of onion in the oil or immerse the tip of a chopstick in the oil. If the onion starts sizzling or if it bubbles immediately around the tip of the chopstick, then it is the right temperature to deep-fry.

Fry in Small Batches
The ideal way to deep-fry is to fry a small amount of food in a large amount of oil. Unfortunately, this is impractical in home cooking since no one wants to be stuck with a big pot of used oil. The alternative would be to use a smaller amount of oil, about 1 to 2 cups and to fry in several batches. When more oil is needed during the frying process, make sure that all the fried foods are taken out of the oil so that they will not turn soggy as the temperature drops suddenly. Store the used oil in a cool place and try to use it soon. Refrigeration is not necessary if it is used within a week.

Close Supervision
As a rule, most deep-frying requires high temperatures. Once the food is added to the hot oil, close supervision is needed. Turn the heat higher when the temperature shows sign of dropping abruptly (this tends to make the food soggy) and turn it lower at the first signs of overheating (this will cause the food to burn). When frying large pieces of meat, use a medium flame. This will allow the food to cook thoroughly. Then turn the heat higher again to create a final golden crust.

Shallow-Frying
This is a popular technique in Chinese cooking and is the counterpart of Western "sautéing." Although shallow-frying is seldom used in the cooking of fancy dishes, it is the most convenient way to cook home meals and some of the popular dim sum dishes. The Chinese shallow-fry marinated meats, fish, pancakes, dumplings, wontons and steamed buns. The aromatic and slightly crunchy taste of these shallow-fried foods is just as marvelous as deep-fried foods. An advantage of shallow-frying is that it is less messy. However, this relatively simple cooking technique demands more supervision and patience than skill. The trick is to use a medium flame and allow the food to brown nicely on one side before turning it to the other side.

Red-Cooking and Flavored Pot
Red-cooking, a popular technique in home cooking, is a sophisticated version of stewing but is seldom used in restaurants because it is a time-consuming cooking technique. The word "red" refers to the color of dark soy sauce and "red-cooking" means cooking meats in sauce. The meat is first browned in oil to seal in the juice and to coat it with a nice aroma; then water (or stock) and seasonings (plenty of soy sauce, spices and herbs) are added. The heat is then set at medium-low for long simmering (1 to 2 hours, depending on the cut).

Tougher cuts of meats are most suitable for this form of cooking. Poultry and fish are also frequently used, but fish requires much less time, 10 to 12 minutes. The red-cooked dishes usually have a deep rich flavor that is highly prized by the Chinese.

The gravy acts as an insulation that slows down the cooling process. For this reason, many expensive Chinese banquet dishes are prepared in this way.

Flavored pot is similar to red cooking in many ways — the use of slow simmering and the addition of soy sauce, herbs and spices. However, flavored pot is simpler (no browning is required) and more versatile; hence it is more popular than red-cooking in households and in restaurants. This may be called the Chinese way of making cold cuts because various kinds of meats (including innards) are cooked in a heavily seasoned rich sauce for about an hour. Then they are sliced paper thin and arranged attractively on a meat platter. These assorted meat slices may be served with sandwiches, at the dinner table, or as the first course of a Chinese banquet.

The biggest advantage of the techniques of red-cooking and flavored pot is that the dishes, which can be made ahead of time, stay fresh in the refrigerator for at least a week. Both cooking methods are ideal ways of preparing foods for parties and picnics and have been widely used by Chinese communities for festivals and social gatherings in this country.

Twice-Cooked Braising

As the name indicates, this involves more than one technique. The meat and vegetables are first stir-fried separately (or deep-fried) and then returned to the wok for flavor blending. This is a dish with plenty of flavorful gravy; hence, stock and seasonings (soy sauce, oyster sauce, pepper, cornstarch, etc.) are added for a subtle taste and smooth consistency. Many Chinese adore this type of dish because it has the aroma of stir-frying and the silky texture of heavy soup.

UTENSILS AND EQUIPMENT

The Rice Cooker

I think every rice lover should applaud the design of the rice cooker that comes to his or her rescue from burnt or undercooked rice. It cooks perfect rice automatically in about 30 minutes, during which time you can leave the kitchen and work in other parts of the house without worrying about burning the rice, for it automatically turns itself off when the rice is done. The rice cooker comes in two parts: the cooker and the inner pan. A simple recipe for cooking rice in the rice cooker is to fill the desired amount of rice in the pan, rinse lightly, add water to one knuckle level above the rice and turn on the red light. A rice cooker is also a perfect steamer. The best part is that it steams food without your supervision.

The Cleaver

A cleaver may look formidable, but it is misleading to assume that it is "dangerous." In fact, with its wide side design and slightly dull blade, a cleaver is rather safe to use. What makes it more efficient is the weight. The weight helps to speed the process and you use less energy than with a regular knife. Certainly, you need some expertise in order to use it correctly. Here is the best way to use the cleaver: hold the cleaver at an angle with your right hand, with the blade tilted slightly outward. This will make beginners feel more comfortable. Once you are used to it, you don't need to hold it outward. Curl the fingers of your left hand like a rake and hold on to the food. Your left hand that is holding the food moves back naturally while the blade cuts away from the fingers.

Once you become accustomed to it, you will find the cleaver a remarkable tool. Aside from cutting meats, vegetables and other food items, this versatile kitchen tool can also be used to pound, crush and carry food. It comes in handy when you are working with pastries — cutting the dough and scraping the board. In restaurants, chefs use different cleavers for different purposes. For home cooks, however, one medium-sized, carbon-steel cleaver will do most of the cutting jobs.

The Cutting Board

A cutting board is a necessity in Chinese cooking. Although some vegetables and meat may be cut by machine, aromatic herbs for sautéing, like ginger, garlic and scallions, are best when cut with a knife on a smooth surface. An ideal cutting board should be large enough to hold the food, convenient to work on and easy to clean. Many home cooks feel that a plastic cutting board meets the above requirements perfectly and is also quite inexpensive. Wash the board well with hot soapy water after each use and dry with a towel.

The Chinese Spatula

This tool is made for Chinese stir-frying. The flat bottom and wide side are perfect for turning, pressing and breaking up lumps in foods. The sharp edge may be used for cutting large pieces of food into smaller sizes (like eggs and pasta). Nothing beats the Chinese spatula for scraping that stubborn residue that adheres to the pan. When transporting food from the wok or pan to the serving plate, you can rely on this tool to do an excellent job. The only disadvantage of the Chinese spatula is that it cannot be used with a nonstick pan.

The Chinese Slotted Spoon

This tool looks like a giant spoon and is excellent for draining foods from oil or water. The Chinese slotted spoons are larger and rounder than the American products and hence are more functional. They come in several sizes and also in two versions: one is made of wire, the other of metal. I prefer the metal one because it is easier to clean. For home cooking, a small one seems to work better. You can find this big spoon distributed by Joyce Chen in some American cookware stores.

Tongs

Tongs are handy for transferring foods from one container to another. They are especially useful for handling ingredients for deep-frying or barbecuing. Not everyone can manipulate a pair of long chopsticks, but a pair of tongs should solve the problem. Tongs are also used for tossing salads, handling ice cubes and serving food at parties. You can find this versatile product in a kitchenware store.

The Strainer (or Colander)

This is a necessity for every kitchen and it is especially important in Chinese cooking. If vegetables are not properly drained with a strainer, you will end up with a bowl of watery salad. For stir-fried dishes, thorough draining of the ingredients is crucial, or the dish will be ruined by excess water. And for cooked noodles and pastas, you need a strainer to wash out excess starch to get a cleaner look and taste. When buying a strainer, my personal advice to the novice is to look for metal or plastic strainers; they work better than wire strainers.

The Wok

A Big Capacity

Although you can stir-fry with a large pan or a skillet, you will find that using a wok makes the cooking job much easier. The dome shape of a wok has a greater capacity than it appears to have. It is almost like a very large mixing bowl that provides more room for turning and tossing. This eliminates splatters and also makes cooking large quantities of leafy vegetables much easier. These vegetables usually shrink to a third of their original bulk — sometimes even less.

Multi-Purpose

Besides stir-frying, a wok is a great deep fryer. The wide rim provides better visibility and easy manipulation and the bowl shape requires less oil in frying, which is another plus factor. To turn a wok into a steamer, you don't even need a rack. Simply fill the wok with 2 to 3 cups of water; place a small heatproof bowl, half filled with water, in the center as a base. Bring the water to a boil and then place the dish to be steamed on top of the heatproof bowl. Just cover and steam.

The Right Size

Woks come in different sizes and materials. Try to look for one that is made of carbon-steel or lightweight iron. Most Chinese home cooks like iron woks because they conduct heat well and foods don't seem to stick to them. How big should a wok be? It depends on your needs. A small one saves space, but a medium one (14 inches) will be more useful when you entertaining.

Cleaning the Wok

A wok requires seasoning only once. After being used for some time, a dark coating forms in the center of the wok and that is actually a natural protection against rust and sticking. It is extremely important to clean (with paper towels) or wash the wok between each stir-frying. A dirty and sticky wok can mess up your dish, affecting both the taste and the appearance. This is how a Chinese home cook handles an oily messy wok after cooking: first scrape the residue (if there is any) with a Chinese spatula (it works better than any other tool) or soak the wok in hot water until the residue loosens up. Wash with dish detergent, using a regular brush or sponge. Dry well and store.

SECRETS IN CHINESE GROCERY STORES

You can cook authentic Chinese dishes without visiting a Chinese market. However, if you have not been to a Chinese market, especially a well-stocked one, you might have missed something invaluable. Even if you live miles away, your trip will be well rewarded because Chinese markets are full of intriguing foodstuffs that will enrich your life. These stores are like a miniature supermarket, delicatessen and take-out eatery, all in one. If you know what to bring home, you can easily have an authentic Chinese dinner party without exhausting yourself with a lot of elaborate cooking. The secret lies in the proper use of convenience foods from the Chinese market.

If you are fortunate enough to come across a good Chinese food market, you are likely to find a whole line of well-prepared and ready-to-serve dishes in the refrigerated section. These Chinese prepared foods have been neatly cut up and packed in small aluminum containers. The mouthwatering range of specialty foods available usually include smoked or roasted ducks, soy sauce chicken, roasted pork, spiced beef, spiced tripe, vegetarian tofu skin, cold tossed seaweed salad, pickled cabbage, tofu salad and so forth.

Recently, many Chinese supermarkets have a mini takeout department selling an array of marvelous tasting hot foods. These well-seasoned prepared dishes usually remain fresh in the refrigerator for at least 4 to 5 days without losing their flavor. They are also extremely affordable. When dining or entertaining at home, you will find hot foods a wonderful convenience, especially when you do not have the time or do not know how to cook a particular dish.

Hot and cold take-out foods are only part of the attraction in Chinese markets. The stores are filled with thousands of interesting food items, from canned products, condiments and sauces to fresh Chinese vegetables, meat products, fresh and frozen seafood, various rice and noodle products, kitchenware, herbal medicines and much more. For many curious Western shoppers, visiting Chinese markets can be educational and even entertaining. Over the years I have brought some of my American neighbors and friends to visit these unique stores. Many of them found the prices of certain food (especially produce, meat and seafood) at these stores to be quite reasonable; others were excited to discover that they could buy ready-cut meats and julienne meats there.

Aside from browsing through the fresh goods in a Chinese market, you should also direct your attention to another section that is too good to be ignored — the frozen dim sum section. Frozen dim sum are convenient to have on hand, easy to reheat and as tasty as freshly made ones. These wonderful convenience foods should not be savored by the Chinese alone but should also be enjoyed by Westerners. Ready-made Chinese dumplings make an excellent substitute for pizzas, hamburgers and sandwiches when you are tired of eating them.

The existence of Chinese markets in this country is a blessing for local people for several reasons: First, the abundance of fresh Chinese vegetables, which are often sought by vegetarians, adds a wonderful dimension to American produce. Second, because of its fast turnover in fresh food supplies, the Chinese markets provide quality products at reasonable prices to customers. This often helps to keep the prices of Asian foods in other stores in check.

The following are just a few

examples of the more popular frozen dim sum available at Chinese supermarkets and that are widely enjoyed by both Chinese and Westerners.

Dumplings
These are inexpensive gourmet food for Chinese households. The popular fillings are pork and cabbage or pork and Chinese chives. They are usually packed in plastic bags with 30 or more in a bag. If you have to travel far in warm weather (for hours at a time), be sure to bring an ice chest to keep the food cold. When completely thawed, uncooked dumplings will stick together and disintegrate during the cooking.

Pork Buns
These are Chinese hot sandwiches. They come in two to three different sizes, ranging from the mini bun to the jumbo meat bun the size of a large orange. The mini bun is extremely juicy inside. The larger buns usually contain a few varieties of fillings (meat, vegetarian or combination). Most of these buns are pre-cooked and ready to serve after being heated briefly. Never boil them in water; microwaving, steaming, baking and sautéing are the best ways to reheat buns.

Sesame Flat Breads
These are layered flat breads, like Middle-Eastern pitas, but with a more refined texture and taste.

There are actually two kinds of sesame flat bread: sweet and savory. Those with sweet fillings are extremely delicious when piping hot and crispy. The savory ones, without fillings, may be eaten plain or used as sandwich bread.

Here are several ways to heat and serve this crispy bread:
* Bake or toast it, but do not steam. Once it becomes soft, the taste is lost.
* Serve it as you would pitas or toasted bread. It tastes great when used as a sandwich.
* Serve it Chinese-style. Stuff it with a fried stick (see Chinese Donut below), or serve with warm soybean milk.

Chinese Donut (Fried Stick)
Most Chinese love to eat this yard-long Chinese donut. This deep-fried savory snack does not really taste like the donut, which is quite sweet. It is crunchy, aromatic and simply delicious!

Heat and serve it in the following ways:
* To reheat — place in a 350°F oven for 5 to 10 minutes; serve it plain.
* To serve in the popular Chinese way — fold one-quarter of a fried stick onto toasted flat bread. Such an aromatic and crunchy sandwich can be a real treat.
* To use as a garnish — cut into thin slices and use as a garnish in your favorite

soups, or as a crunchy bed for your stir-fried dishes.

Sweet Rice Dumplings
Shaped like ping-pong balls, this traditional festival food (for the New Year) has now become an all-year-round popular dessert. Three kinds of fillings are available at the Chinese markets: red bean paste, sesame paste and creamy peanuts. The Chinese usually boil them with 4 to 5 cups of water and serve warm (some people like to add slices of ginger and a few tablespoons of sugar for added flavor). You can also serve them in the following fashion: steam for 8 to 10 minutes, then cool to room temperature; serve with maple syrup or your favorite sweet sauce.

Scallion Pancakes
This layered pancake originated from Northern China and was so well liked that it became a national favorite. A perfect scallion pancake should be eaten on the same day it is made. Nowadays, we have the good fortune to enjoy scallion cakes without having to make them ourselves — frozen scallion pancakes are available in most Chinese food markets. The best way to reheat is to allow them to brown slowly over medium-high heat on a well-greased pan until both sides are crisp. Serve plain or with meat and vegetables, pizza-style.

DINING IN A DIM SUM HOUSE

You don't have to spend a fortune to enjoy a Chinese feast. You can indulge in a sumptuous Chinese meal by dining at a good dim sum house. Once you have tasted the staggering variety of foods served in dim sum houses, you will understand why flocks of Chinese diners are attracted to these places daily (some dim sum houses serve dim sum brunch only on weekends). My American friends liken a dim sum lunch to a cocktail party, without the cocktail, and also to a non-stop buffet. Whatever you like to call it, the wonderful style of dim sum dining is unique to Chinese cuisine.

The art of Chinese cooking is exemplified in dim sum preparations. Every morsel of the delicate looking dumplings, rolls and balls is a work of art — reminiscent of the jade carved figures in a museum. And the unusual way in which it is presented further enhances the dining atmosphere.

"Dim sum" in Chinese literally means "to delight one's heart" and the foods in a dim sum house are truly a joy to behold. On each wheeled cart, pushed by a vending lady who occasionally announces the names of the dim sum, three to five different items are stacked separately for convenient selection. Pastries and buns look especially attractive in their lovely little bamboo and tin containers. In a smaller dim sum house you can expect a selection of 35 to 40 different varieties, whereas in a larger place you will have over 80 items to choose from, excluding the regular dishes on the menu. It is the stunning diversity of bite-sized foods in a dim sum house that appeals to Chinese from all regions and has captivated even the hearts of diners from other nations.

The beauty of dim sum dining, however, is not in the variety alone. It is also an economical and fun way to sample Chinese food. When ordering from a menu in a regular restaurant, without first seeing the actual dishes, you will probably have to ponder long and hard to find the ideal combination, lest you waste money on dishes you won't enjoy. In a dim sum house you can be more relaxed since you choose the foods that appeal to you most straight from the pushcarts. If you make a mistake in your selection, the dish will only cost you from two to five dollars, a fraction of what the regular dishes on the menu cost. For a party of two, you can literally indulge in a ten-course feast without spending a fortune and still have leftovers to take home.

If you are a novice at dim sum dining and would like to get the best result on your first visit to a dim sum house, you will find these tips and guidelines extremely helpful.
* First, try to locate the best dim sum house near you. A good dim sum house not only provides a larger selection of dim sum but also offers better quality as well.
* Second, since a dim sum lunch is a hearty meal, it would be wise to limit your breakfast to a minimum or to omit it completely. Also, do not fill yourself up with the first two or three courses. You need to save room for the delicacies that continue to come your way. If the pieces are too big, cut them in halves and share with your partners. Leftovers may be taken home and reheated the

following day.

* Third, if you want to try a great variety of dishes, go with a group of friends or relatives. Four to six people (or more) in a group will provide the chance to sample more foods. Besides the dim sum dishes on the pushcart, you can also order fried noodles, seafood and vegetable dishes on the menu to share with the group.

Since most dim sum vendors don't speak enough English to introduce the foods they sell, try to go with a Chinese friend who can be your interpreter. If you are truly serious about your visit to the dim sum house, perhaps you should do a little research in advance. Go to your local library or bookstore and look through some books on Chinese dim sum.

Recently I have had the most enjoyable dim sum dining experience in Taiwan. The restaurant not only included Northern-style appetizers, which rarely appear in an ordinary dim sum house, but also provided a nice variety of vegetarian dishes such as vegetable-filled dumplings, zesty pickles, crunchy stir-fried dishes. I thought the restaurant was a fine example for dim sum houses in other places to emulate.

These days, people are not so hungry for a meal dominated by meat. On the contrary, many health enthusiasts are in constant search of good vegetarian dishes. I believe that dim sum dining would be more alluring to Western diners if restaurants could display an array of tasty vegetable dishes in their pushcarts.

The following short descriptions of the most popular dim sum dishes savored by the Chinese may give you some clue as to what to choose the next time you are in a dim sum house.

Chinese Radish Cake and Taro Cake

This tender, fragrant cake is made from rice flour and the long white radish you see in supermarkets. Chinese sausage and scallions are added to intensify the flavor. Before serving, the cake is usually cut into squares and sautéed until slightly crusty and golden brown. This heavenly cake pleases everyone because the good taste lingers. In some dim sum houses you might also find taro cake, which is slightly different from Chinese radish cake, but equally delicious.

Shrimp Dumplings

Transparent and beautifully shaped, these delicate mini dumplings are filled with sweet tender shrimp and crunchy bamboo shoots. Unlike the skins of other dumplings, which are made with wheat flour, the skins of shrimp dumplings are made from a combination of wheat starch and cornstarch, which gives them a whiter color and a more tender texture.

Shao Mai

These are open-faced steamed meat dumplings shaped like vases. The fillings of Shao Mai vary with restaurants. The popular filling ingredients are pork, beef, shrimp and sticky rice mixed with a small amount of water chestnuts.

Fried Shrimp Balls

The taste of fried shrimp balls is marvelous. It is delicate, bouncy and chewy on the inside, aromatic and crisp on the outside. The best tasting shrimp balls are coated with breadcrumbs or rice noodle puffs. For some reason this delicacy is not available in every dim sum house. If you happen to find them on the pushcarts, seize and enjoy them.

Fried Taro Dumplings

Taro root emits a wonderful chestnut-like aroma when freshly cooked. It is no wonder why fried taro dumplings with meat fillings are so popular with diners. Extremely soft on the inside, crispy and fragrant on the outside, this deep-fried morsel offers an array of tastes and textures. A word of warning about taro dumplings — they are heavy and filling, so don't eat too much before you taste other dim sum.

Pork Buns

These are meat-filled buns that come in two or three varieties. Barbecued pork buns have a slightly sweet and juicy filling made solely from barbecued pork. Other pork buns might be filled with a combination of ground pork, chicken and vegetables. Choose the smaller buns because they usually taste better than the larger ones. If you don't like the fluffy white pork buns, try the baked buns which resemble French rolls (with pork filling). Since these are rather filling, you might want to share one with someone else.

Curry Beef Pastry

Although curry powder is not a popular spice in Chinese cooking, curry beef pies are well liked by many diners. The tender and juicy beef filling is encased in a flaky and crusty skin. It is

something that a curry and pie lover should not miss.

Tofu Skin Rolls

Tofu skin rolls, along with Chinese radish cake (turnip cake), are at the top of my personal list of favorites. The smooth pork filling may taste the same as the filling in other dumplings, but when wrapped in a layer of tofu skin, it turns into a stunningly delicious morsel. This is because the tofu skin has been fried and then steamed, adding a delicate texture and a rich taste to the dish.

Spring Rolls

Spring Rolls in a dim sum house are usually higher in quality than those of other restaurants. The difference between a good Spring Roll and a poorly made one lies in both the skin and the filling. A well-made Spring Roll is tender, juicy and flavorful on the inside, and delicately crisp on the outside. Tasty fillings include meat, shrimp, cabbage and bamboo shoots. Do not look for large sizes. In most cases, smaller ones taste better.

Creamy Rice Congee

Years ago this was a poor man's meal, but the Cantonese made it so palatable that the taste rivals some of the best

tasting soups. The ingredients for basic congee are rather simple: rice, meat stock, dried seafood and minced ginger. Occasionally, tofu skin is added. Once the basic congee is cooked, other ingredients such as beef, fish slices or assorted meats are added to enrich the flavor. Congee tastes best when served with crispy pastries such as fried sticks. For those who have not tasted congee before, I recommend that you try beef congee or sliced fish congee.

Sesame Balls

These are the favorite desserts of Western diners. They are made from sticky rice flour dough, filled with sweet red bean paste, coated with sesame seeds and then deep-fried to a golden brown. They taste wonderful while they are hot and crispy. They are creamy on the inside, and tender, chewy and fragrant on the outside, a rather intriguing product for pastry lovers.

DUMPLINGS, NOODLES AND RICE

The Story of Dumplings

Almost every cuisine has some form of dumpling, but the dazzling variety of Chinese dumplings is a culinary phenomenon. There are hundreds of recipes. In a broad sense, any filled dough could be called a dumpling, but here I would like to focus my discussion on the half-moon dumpling, which is called "Jiao Zi" by the Chinese and "pot sticker" by some Westerners.

The Chinese have enjoyed eating dumplings for more than two thousand years, but very few people know the touching story behind the origin of meat dumplings. Tradition has it that a prominent Chinese herbalist, Zhang Zhong Jing of the Han Dynasty (25-220), who was known for his medical skills and charitable deeds, inspired the invention of the modern dumpling. During the harsh winter months of Northern China, when many impoverished people suffered from severe frostbite, the kind herbal doctor established a relief station where healing herb dumplings were distributed to the victims. These dumplings, stuffed with mutton, chili and various herbs, worked wonders for frostbite and saved hundreds of lives. Since then, meat dumplings have become the hallmark of Northern Chinese food.

Propelled by modern refrigeration, meat dumplings are rapidly becoming a popular snack and a convenience food for the Chinese people throughout the world. Even with the competition from Western fast food, it is still a fast growing convenience food in Chinese homes. I would not be surprised if its popularity is also spreading to households of other cultures. There are good reasons why dumplings continue to thrive in a busy modern world. To begin with, dumplings can provide a complete meal. With a juicy, meaty filling (vegetables are usually added too) and a smooth flavorful skin, this "Chinese ravioli" is thoroughly satisfying as a savory snack as well as a filling staple. The Northern Chinese consider its taste comparable to even the most elegant banquet dishes and as such, it has become a tradition to serve dumplings on festive occasions, or when entertaining.

In addition, the meat dumplings are most flexible in terms of fillings. Although pork and beef are the popular main ingredients, vegetables such as napa cabbage, Chinese chives, daikon or green beans are invariably added to lighten the taste and to balance the nutrition. Meatless vegetarian dumplings with a lighter and healthier filling were created to delight vegetarians. Cellophane noodles, mushrooms and pressed tofu are frequently used in vegetarian dumplings. High in flavor, but low in calories, vegetarian dumplings may well be the "dream food" for the health conscious.

On top of all these assets, making meat dumplings can be surprisingly economical. The actual cost of the ingredients for each dumpling is just pennies, a great advantage when you want a gourmet meal on a budget. However, you need to be able to judge the quality of dumplings, whether you buy or make them. A good filling should be smooth, juicy, subtle and aromatic tasting.

The skin should feel soft and smooth but elastic. If you are thinking of learning to make the dumplings yourself, try to learn from a cooking demonstration, or better yet from a Chinese friend who is experienced in making dumplings. This is something that truly requires a certain amount of skill and practice. But once you have mastered this special skill, you'll enjoy making dumplings for the rest of your life.

Making dumplings at home can be a rewarding team project and a recreational one when you have the time. But with today's busy life style, even the skillful Chinese housewife must sometimes rely on buying frozen dumplings, a trend that Western shoppers are following. At Chinese markets, I have seen people from other cultures buying bags of dumplings. An American shopper revealed that her life has been made simpler since she discovered the "Chinese fast food"— frozen meat dumplings. She usually buys two large bags consisting of 100 pieces at one time, then cooks them in 4 batches in boiling water. When the boiled dumplings are cool, she packs them in individual bags and freezes them for a quick meal or a snack.

Speaking of cooking

dumplings, here is a little anecdote that you might find amusing. An American couple fell in love with meat dumplings while visiting Taiwan. Painstakingly, they learned every detail about making meat dumplings and were successful in wrapping them up just as they were taught. Now came the final step — boiling dumplings in water. To their disappoint-ment and dismay, the dumplings turned into a pot of mushy stew. Their first thought was to blame the water and flour for their failure. After much inquiry, they found the reason for their failure — dumplings should never be cooked in cold water and that was exactly what they had done to their dumplings. So you have learned an important rule: always bring the water to a boil before adding the pot sticker meat dumplings.

Wontons
Wontons are another delicate and subtle tasting form of dumplings, which delight native Chinese as well as Westerners. The word "wonton," which is the romanization of its Cantonese name, means "swallowing the cloud." And that is exactly how a good wonton soup should taste. Unfortunately, with today's labor costs, truly impressive

wonton soups (by Chinese gourmet standards) are very hard to come by. Thus, Chinese home cooks in this country feel that instead of driving miles to Chinatown for a bowl of wonton soup, the most reliable way to enjoy good wontons is to make them at home. Making wontons is actually easier than making other dumplings.

The following guidelines will certainly be of help if you are interested in making them yourself.

* Select very fresh ground pork loin since the taste of this dish depends largely on the quality of the meat. Adding a small portion of minced fresh shrimp or crabmeat will give the filling a subtler and sweeter taste. For vegetable lovers, using a small portion of vegetables (napa cabbage or mushrooms) will add a nice refreshing taste.

* Use quality pork bones or chicken legs to make a super stock since the stock counts as half of the goodness of wonton soup. A short cut to producing a good stock is simply to boil a few pieces of spareribs in chicken broth. These two combine to create an exceptionally tasty stock.

* Garnish your wonton soup

with mixed chopped herbs of celery, scallions and cilantro (adding a little chopped pickled Sichuan mustard green is even better). These green garnishes add a wonderful aroma to the soup.

Noodles and Rice

Both rice and noodles are staples in China. In some households, rice is eaten more often than noodles while the reverse is true in other households. It all depends on where people grew up. Generally, the Chinese like to have rice for dinner; noodles are usually taken for lunch or as a filling snack. However, this rule can vary occasionally. Unlike rice, which is eaten along with various dishes, noodles are basically a one-dish meal, often served all by itself. But Chinese noodles are never boring — many of them are quite elaborate, topped with lots of meat and vegetables. When you order lo-mein noodles in a restaurant, you have probably seen beef, chicken or seafood lo-mein on the menu. Even in a bowl of cold noodles, sauces and herbs are not the only seasonings. Crunchy vegetables such as cucumbers or bean sprouts are added for additional texture. Sometimes, aromatic roasted meats are added as toppings to boost the flavor of the cold noodles.

One popular form of noodles that most Chinese adore is the soup noodle. Soup noodle is a complete meal in itself — there is starch, meat and vegetables, all in a bowl of very flavorful soup. Its taste is extremely satisfying and soothing, perhaps the best you can expect from a one-dish meal. The basic rules for making delicious soup noodle are quite similar to that of wonton soup — you need well-flavored broth, aromatic rich toppings and of course, quality noodles. Limited by space, I have included only one soup noodle dish in this chapter. But I would strongly recommend that you try a variety of soup noodles in a good restaurant, especially the Sichuan spicy beef noodle soup and the Cantonese seafood noodle soup. Sichuan beef noodle soup has such a tantalizing taste that it seems to please everyone in Taiwan. In Taipei, you are likely to find a beef noodle shop on almost every block. And even on this continent, in Chinese neighborhoods, Sichuan beef noodle soup is the specialty of many noodle shops.

* * * * * * *

For centuries, rice has been considered a life-sustaining grain in China. This is often reflected in Chinese daily language. For instance, when asking about someone's job, one could say, "What kind of rice does he eat?" to mean what kind of job does he hold. Today, rice has finally been recognized as a healthful and tasty staple by Westerners and is gaining popularity. Indeed, no other staple goes so well with every kind of dish as rice does. This may explain why the Chinese have such a passion for stir-fried vegetables — because white rice makes them taste great.

Despite a stunning variety of rice dishes in Chinese cookery, Westerners seem to favor only fried rice, which is not considered a great dish by the Chinese. If you truly enjoy fried rice, I suggest that you try the best version — seafood fried rice, also called "Yangzhou (Young Chow) Fried Rice." I also encourage rice lovers to try a few uniquely delicious sticky rice dishes — Rice Dumpling in Bamboo Leaves (Zong Zi), Fried Sticky Rice, or Steamed Rice in Lotus Leaves. There is a deep, rich taste in these dishes that has no equal. More discussion on rice may be found in the Glossary of Ingredients.

餃子
Meat Dumplings

Meat dumplings have finally caught the fancy of Westerners. Many Western gourmets are learning how to make meat dumplings. This is an excellent idea because homemade dumplings are fresher and often tastier. It is fun to make these half-moon meat pockets from scratch, together with a group of friends. If you have difficulty in making wrappers, don't be discouraged. Simply buy the ready-to-use dumpling wrappers in Chinese stores.

Dough

3 cups unbleached all-
  purpose flour
1 cup water

Filling

1 1/4 cups ground pork or
  turkey
1 1/2 cups chopped celery or
  napa cabbage stems
1/2 cup chopped onion

Marinade

2 tablespoons soy sauce
2 teaspoons dry sherry
1/2 teaspoon salt
1 tablespoon sesame oil
2 tablespoons cornstarch
  pepper to taste
1/4 teaspoon five-spice
  powder (optional)

Dipping Sauce

2 tablespoons soy sauce
2 tablespoons vinegar
2 teaspoons sesame oil
1 teaspoon minced garlic
  (optional)

Method

1. To make the dough: Place flour in a medium-sized mixing bowl and make a well in the center. Pour half the water into the well and start mixing with a fork, gradually adding the rest of the water to form a soft dough. Place the dough in a plastic bag and let it rest for at least 15 minutes. This will make the dough smoother and easier to work.

2. To make the filling: In another bowl, combine the pork, celery and onion with the marinade. Mix thoroughly to make a flavorful filling.

3. To make the skin: Work the dough on a lightly floured surface until smooth, about 2 minutes. Make a hole in the center of the dough and stretch it out into a long sausage, about 2/3-inch in diameter.

Cut the "sausage" into 2 parts. Cover one part with a plastic bag to keep it from drying while you work on the other part. Use a kitchen knife and cut the long dough into mini-dough pieces the size of a cherry. Flatten each piece, dusting lightly with flour to prevent sticking. Repeat with the rest of the dough.

4. Now comes the crucial part of making the dumpling wrappers. Lay the palm of your right hand, with your fingers wide apart, on the rolling pin. Hold the mini-dough with your left hand and rotate it slowly in a circular motion while you use your right hand simultaneously to push the rolling pin forward to press the edge of the dough. Continue to rotate and press the dough until

you get a circle about 2 inches (or less) in diameter. The center should be 2~3 times thicker than the edge so that it will hold the filling better. When the dough gets sticky, simply dust it with a little flour. Repeat with the rest of the pieces and spread out the circles to keep them from sticking together.

5. To wrap the dumplings: Hold a piece of wrapper in your left hand, place 1 teaspoon of filling in the center, then fold the edge of the wrapper over the filling. Pinch the top part of the curved edges together then make 2 pleats along each side of the curved edge to make a neat half-moon dumpling. Place the dumplings on a lightly floured cookie sheet.

6. In a medium-sized stockpot, bring half a pot of water to a rolling boil. Drop the dumplings gently into the water, one or two at a time, adding no more than 25 in one batch. Using the back of a metal spatula (to avoid breaking the dumplings with the sharp part), stir lightly to prevent sticking. Cook, uncovered, for 10~12 minutes over medium-high heat. Turn the heat off and remove the dumplings to a serving bowl. Serve warm with the dipping sauce.

Makes 30~40 dumplings

Variation
For an even tastier version, sauté dumplings with oil in small batches until both sides turn brown.

Note
Use a thin rolling pin with a diameter of 2/3 inch. You can buy this at large Chinese food markets.

牛肉餡餅
Crispy Beef Pancake

This aromatic dumpling pancake used to be a very popular street food in China a few decades back. Oddly enough, it is not easy to find it nowadays except in some Shanghai or Northern Chinese restaurants. This pancake is almost like a beef hamburger wrapped in crusty dough. The nice part is that the beef filling is juicier than a hamburger's. And the taste is quite close to "American's," as one of my neighbors says.

oil for sautéing
3/4 cup water
1 teaspoon sesame oil

Dough
3 cups all-purpose flour
1 cup plus 1 tablespoon hot
   water

Filling
3/4 pound tender cut of
   ground beef
2 tablespoons rice wine or
   dry sherry
2 tablespoons soy sauce
1 tablespoon sesame oil
1/2 tablespoon sugar
1/3 teaspoon five-spice
   powder
1/2 teaspoon black pepper
   salt to taste
1/4 cup cornstarch
1 1/2 cups diced onion
1/2 cup chopped celery

Method
1. To make the dough: Place the flour in a large mixing bowl and make a well in the center. Add about half of the hot water to the flour, mixing gently with a fork. Gradually add the rest of the water and continue to blend the flour into a soft dough. Place the dough in a plastic bag and let rest for at least 30 minutes.

2. To make the filling: In another mixing bowl, mix the beef with the rice wine, soy sauce, sesame oil, sugar, five-spice powder, black pepper, salt and cornstarch; marinate for 10 minutes. Add the onion and celery to the marinated beef and mix well with a fork until thoroughly blended.

3. To form the beef pancakes: Set the filling and dough on a smooth kitchen table. Knead the dough for 1~2 minutes until it holds together. Divide the dough into 3 portions, return two to the bag (to prevent dryness) and work on one. Roll the dough into a long sausage and cut into 12~14 pieces. Using a thin rolling pin, roll each piece into a round about 2 1/2 inches in diameter, with the center slightly thicker than the rim. Place 1 tablespoon of filling in the center, gather the edges together and pinch to seal in the center. Repeat with the rest of dough and filling. Place the beef dumpling pancakes on a large plate or a baking sheet lined with plastic wrap (to prevent sticking).

Cook just enough for the day and freeze the rest for future use.

4. To cook the beef pancakes: Before turning the heat on, grease a large pan with enough oil to coat and add about 10 beef cakes to it. Turn the heat to medium high and lightly brown both sides. Add about 3/4 cup of water and 1 teaspoon sesame oil to the beef cakes. Cover and simmer over medium heat for about 8 minutes or until the water dries out completely. Flip the cakes over and continue to cook until both sides are brown and crusty. Remove to a serving plate. Beef pancakes must be eaten within 10 minutes before they lose their crispiness.

Makes 38~40 pancakes

春捲
Spring Rolls

Almost half the taste of Spring Rolls comes from the crust; the rest comes from a tender juicy flavorful filling. As long as they are well seasoned and carefully cooked, vegetables can taste wonderful with just a little lift from a small amount of meat. This is the idea behind this recipe. Isn't this a good way to serve vegetables to someone who normally doesn't eat them?

 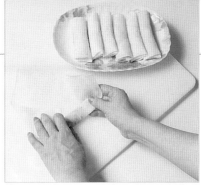 

2/3 pound ground pork
1/4 cup oil for stir-frying
1 tablespoon chopped garlic
2 tablespoons chopped
  scallions, white and green
  parts separated
1 1/2 cups finely sliced napa
  cabbage
1 cup finely shredded carrots
1 cup finely shredded
  potatoes
1 package (25 pieces)
  imported thin Spring Roll
  wrappers
1 egg, beaten
2-3 cups oil for deep-frying

Marinade
1 tablespoon soy sauce
2 teaspoons dry sherry
1 tablespoon cornstarch

Seasoning Sauce
1 tablespoon oyster sauce
1 teaspoon sesame oil
salt and pepper to taste
1 teaspoon chili paste
1/4 cup chicken broth

Method
1. To make the filling: Mix
   the ground pork with the
   marinade and let stand for
   10 minutes. Heat 1/4 cup
   of oil over medium heat
   and stir-fry the marinated
   pork until the color
   changes. Remove.

2. Reheat the oil. Saute the
   garlic and the white part
   of the scallions until light
   brown. Stir-fry the
   cabbage and carrots for 2-3
   minutes; add the pork and
   potatoes and stir
   thoroughly for 1 minute to
   coat with flavor. Add the
   seasoning sauce and keep
   tossing for another 2
   minutes to prevent the
   potatoes from sticking to
   the pan. Add the rest of
   the scallions and remove to
   a bowl. Let cool to room
   temperature.

3. To assemble the Spring
   Rolls: Set up an assembly
   line on the kitchen table.
   Place a wrapper on the
   table with one corner
   facing you; place about 1
   1/2 tablespoon of filling
   near the corner and shape
   it like a sausage. Wrap the
   filling tightly as though
   you are wrapping a
   package — bring both
   corners on the side to the
   center and roll it up until
   the end. Seal with the
   beaten egg. Sometimes the
   wrapper becomes too dry
   and does not seal properly.
   To resolve this problem,
   you can make a
   tablespoonful of starch
   glue by cooking a little
   cornstarch solution. This
   glue will definitely do a
   better job than the egg.

4. To deep-fry the Spring
   Rolls: Heat 2~3 cups of oil
   and deep-fry the Spring
   Rolls in small batches
   until golden brown. Serve
   immediately. For best
   results, serve the fried
   Spring Rolls on the same
   day. Allow 2 per person.
   Freeze the rest of the
   Spring Rolls for future use.

Makes 25 rolls

蔥油大餅
Fried Scallion Bread

The classic scallion pancake is a great dish except for its short-lived crispness. To remedy this pitfall, I prefer to use another Northern version, which has all the good flavor of scallion pancakes but retains its crispness longer and reheats well. I usually make it a few days in advance and deep-fry just before serving. To have a more interesting presentation, I sometimes make a batch in heart shapes and use them as a garnish.

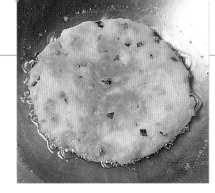

2 cups Bisquick cake mix
3 cups all-purpose flour
3/4 cup chopped scallions
2/3 cup sugar
1 large egg, beaten
1 tablespoon baking powder
2 tablespoons corn oil
3/4 cup water at room
　　temperature
oil for shallow-frying

Method

1. In a mixing bowl, combine all the ingredients. Mix with a spatula until the dough is formed. The dough should be soft but not sticky. Add more flour if necessary. Work the dough on a board or kitchen table until slightly smooth, about 1 minute. The dough need not be as smooth as bread dough.

2. Divide the dough into 4~5 portions. Roll each portion into a small circle like a pizza. Place the circles on separate cookie sheets and bake at 300°F for 20~25 minutes or until light brown and firm. Remove from the oven. You may skip this step if you plan to serve on the same day. The purpose of baking the scallion bread is to make it easier to store and to reheat.

3. Heat 1/2 cup of oil over high heat. Shallow-fry the scallion pancakes, one at a time, until light golden brown. Immediately remove to a tray lined with paper towels to absorb excess oil and then cut into wedges. For best results fry enough for eating on the same day. Refrigerate the rest for future use.

Makes 4~5 pieces

雞絲湯麵

Soup Noodles with Chicken

Soup noodles provide a complete meal with satisfying taste for those on the move. This noodle dish contains mixed meat, greens, noodles and a very soothing broth. The rule of thumb in cooking tasty soup noodles is to select good-quality Chinese noodles. And bear in mind that Chinese noodles cook in much less time than American pasta. They should retain their silky and resilient texture and not become sticky during cooking. Good broth and tasty garnishes are a must for great tasting soup noodles.

1/2~2/3 pound chicken breast
1 bunch baby bok choy or
   watercress
1 pound white noodles, fresh
   or dried noodles
2 cups chicken broth
2 cups water
1/2 cup shredded Canadian
   bacon (optional)
1 tablespoon sesame oil
salt and pepper to taste

Marinade

1 tablespoon soy sauce
1 teaspoon dry sherry
1 tablespoon cornstarch
1 teaspoon sesame oil
1/2 egg white, beaten
1 teaspoon scallions

Garnish

2 tablespoons chopped
   scallions
2 tablespoons cilantro

Method

1. Cut the chicken breast
   into thin strips and mix
   with the marinade; let
   stand for 2~3 minutes.
   Rinse the baby bok choy
   well.

2. In a large stewing pot,
   bring approximately 2/3
   pot of water to a rolling
   boil. Add the noodles to the
   boiling water, stirring
   gently to prevent sticking.
   Cook for 3~5 minutes.
   Since cooking time varies
   with brands, check the
   noodles after 3 minutes to
   see if they are done. The
   noodles should be tender
   but still elastic. Turn off
   the heat and allow the
   noodles to finish cooking in
   the hot liquid.

3. In the meantime, pour the
   chicken broth and water (2
   cups) into a medium-sized
   pot and bring to a boil.
   Add the Canadian bacon
   and baby bok choy. When
   it comes to a boil again,
   add the chicken strips,
   stirring lightly to mix with
   the broth. As soon as the
   soup boils again, turn off
   the heat.

4. When serving, use a
   medium bowl (about 16~20
   ounces) and fill half the
   bowl with noodles; then
   pour enough broth to cover
   the noodles, topping with
   chicken strips, baby bok
   choy, lots of garnish, also
   sprinkle of sesame oil, salt
   and pepper. If you like
   noodles with a zesty taste,
   add a little more pepper or
   chili bean paste.

2~4 servings

餛飩湯
Wonton Soup

Although a good filling and thin wonton skins are essential for the success of wonton soup, the broth itself is just as important. A few pieces of spareribs and garnishing herbs in the chicken broth will enhance its flavor greatly. If properly cooked, your homemade wonton soup will taste better than the ones you find in a lot of noodle shops in the United States.

1/2 package wonton skin

Soup Base
4 cups chicken broth
6 cups water
2 strips (about 1/2 pound)
    spareribs or pork bones

Wonton Filling
1/2 cup chopped napa
    cabbage stem or celery
1/2 pound ground pork
1 tablespoon soy sauce
1 teaspoon sesame oil
1 teaspoon salt
1 tablespoon chopped
    scallions

Garnish
few stalks watercress
3 tablespoons chopped
    scallions
1 tablespoon Sichuan
    mustard green (optional)
1 tablespoon sesame oil
salt and pepper to taste

Method
1. To make the soup base:
   Boil all the soup base
   ingredients, uncovered,
   over medium-high heat for
   15-20 minutes or until

flavorful. Skim off and
discard the scum. Turn off
the heat, remove the
spareribs and keep them
for other uses.

2. To make the filling:
   Squeeze out the water
   from the cabbage and put
   them in a bowl. Add the
   ground pork, soy sauce,
   sesame oil, salt and
   scallions. Mix thoroughly
   to make a smooth filling.

3. To wrap the wontons:
   Place a wonton skin in
   your hand and put about 1
   teaspoon of filling in the
   center. Wet the edges of
   the skin with water then
   fold over the filling to
   make a triangle. Pinch the
   outer corners together so
   that they overlap all the
   way down. The filled
   triangle should now
   resemble a paper hat.
   Repeat with the rest of the
   wonton skin and filling.

4. To cook the wontons: Bring
   the broth to a boil again

and add more water, if
necessary, to keep the pot
at two-thirds full. Add half
the wontons and cook for
about 5 minutes. Do not
crowd the pot with too
many wontons because
wonton soup tastes better
with plenty of broth. When
the wontons are cooked,
add the garnish and turn
off the heat immediately.
Serve hot.

6~8 servings

Variation
Sautéed wontons. Cook
wontons briefly in chicken
broth, about 2 minutes, then
drain well. In a frying pan,
heat 2 tablespoons of oil over
medium-high heat. Carefully
lower the cooked wontons
into the hot oil and sauté
until both sides are nicely
browned; remove to a serving
platter. This is a wonderful
finger food for parties.

炸 醬 麵

Noodles with Savory Meat Sauce

This popular dish is loaded with zing and there are many versions of it: Beijing, Shanghai, Sichuan and Taiwanese. I like them all, so I combined the seasonings from the various versions in one sauce. This is an easy and convenient dish to cook because the sauce can be prepared beforehand. Make a few jars of the sauce — freeze some and refrigerate some — and you will be able to enjoy many meals of tasty noodles or spaghetti without much fuss.

2 medium carrots
2 medium Kirby cucumbers
2 squares of pressed tofu
  (optional)
1 large onion
1 pound lean ground pork
oil for sautéing
4-6 cloves garlic, crushed
salt and pepper to taste
1 tablespoon oyster sauce
2 teaspoons Sichuan
  peppercorns
1 pound dried Chinese
  noodles
2 tablespoons chopped
  scallions for garnish

Marinade

2 teaspoons dry sherry
1 tablespoon soy sauce
1 tablespoon cornstarch
Pepper to taste

Seasonings

2 tablespoons sweet bean
  sauce or Hoisin sauce
2 teaspoons hot chili bean
  paste (optional)
1 tablespoon soy sauce
1 tablespoon sugar

Method

1. To make the meat sauce:
   Rinse the carrots and
   cucumbers lightly. Peel the
   carrots and cut into cubes.
   Do not peel the cucumbers
   but remove any black
   spots on the skin. Cut the
   tofu and onion into cubes
   to match the carrot cubes.

2. Add the marinade to the
   pork and mix well. For a

multi-flavor recipe like
this, you don't need to
marinate the pork for too
long, but using marinade
makes the meat smoother
and juicier.

3. Heat 2 tablespoons of oil
   over high heat. Sauté half
   the garlic and a few pieces
   of onion until fragrant.
   Immediately add the
   carrots and the rest of the
   onion (save a few pieces of
   onion for the pork),
   stirring quickly to mix
   with hot oil. Sprinkle salt
   and pepper to taste, cook
   for about 2 minutes, then
   add the cucumbers and
   oyster sauce. Continue
   tossing to blend the flavors
   together, 2~3 minutes.
   Remove and set aside.

4. Wash the wok and dry
   well. Heat 3 tablespoons of
   oil over medium-high heat
   until very hot. Turn off the
   heat and drop the Sichuan
   peppercorns in the hot oil.
   Allow them to sizzle a few
   seconds to extract the
   flavor. Discard the
   peppercorns with a clean
   spoon.

5. Reheat the oil over
   medium-high heat and
   brown the rest of the garlic
   and onion. Add the sweet
   bean sauce, stirring lightly
   to bring out the flavor.
   Now add the pork to the
   very fragrant oil, tossing

gently to mix with the oil
and to break the lumps
into bits. Add the hot chili
bean paste (if you like the
peppery taste), the soy
sauce and sugar. Mix well.

6. Return the vegetables to
   the wok and toss the
   ingredients together. By
   now the sauce should be
   very rich and flavorful.
   Remove to a large bowl.
   Serve a small portion, 1~2
   cups, with noodles and
   save the rest for future
   use.

7. To cook the noodles: In a
   large stewing pot, bring
   approximately 2/3 pot of
   water to a rolling boil. Add
   the noodles to the boiling
   water, stirring gently to
   prevent sticking. Cook for
   3~5 minutes. Since
   cooking time varies with
   brands, check the noodles
   after 3 minutes to see if
   they are done. The noodles
   should be tender but still
   elastic. Turn off the heat
   and allow the noodles to
   finish cooking in the hot
   liquid.

8. To serve: Spoon a portion
   of noodles in a serving
   bowl, then top with half a
   cup of meat sauce and
   garnish with some
   scallions. Toss well and
   serve hot.

6-8 servings

川味涼麵
Sichuan-Style Cold Noodles

My guests have rated this recipe the best version of meatless cold noodles. The robust taste of the noodle sauce is the result of blending various potent seasonings with flavorful herbs. This is an appetizing dish for cookouts and picnics.

1 pound dried Chinese
  noodles
1 tablespoon oil for tossing
  noodles

Sauce

1 teaspoon minced ginger
2 tablespoons chopped garlic
1 tablespoon chopped
  scallions
3 tablespoons peanut butter
2 tablespoon corn oil
2 tablespoons sesame oil
2 tablespoons soy sauce
2 tablespoons vinegar
2 tablespoons sugar
1 tablespoon dry sherry
salt to taste
1 teaspoon chili bean paste
  or hot oil (optional)
1/2 cup chopped celery,
  strings removed
1/2 cup crushed roasted
  peanuts (optional)

Method

1. To cook the noodles: In a large soup pot, add water to fill halfway and bring to a rolling boil. Add the noodles in 2 batches, stirring lightly to prevent sticking. Cook for about 3 minutes but not more than 5 minutes. Pour the entire pot of noodles into a strainer and rinse with cold water to stop further cooking. The noodles should be soft but still resilient. Transfer the noodles to a large mixing bowl; add the oil (1 tablespoon) and toss lightly so they will not stick together.

2. To make the sauce: In a medium-sized bowl, combine the ginger, garlic and scallions and spread the peanut butter on top. Heat the corn oil and drizzle on the peanut butter to melt it. Add the rest of sauce ingredients and mix well.

3. To serve: Diners help themselves by putting one portion (about 1 cup) of the cold noodles on a plate or a medium bowl and adding about 1 tablespoon of sauce on top. Toss to mix well. Leftovers may be refrigerated.

2~4 servings

炒米粉

Stir-Fried Rice Sticks

This is a well-liked Southern noodle dish. There are many advantages of using rice sticks. They require just a few minutes of soaking in warm water before stir-frying. The light taste and texture of rice sticks make it possible for this dish to retain flavor even after it cools, and this is an asset when it comes to outdoor dining.

1 (1~pound) package rice sticks (available in Chinese stores)
1 pound lean pork, cut into thin strips
oil for stir-frying
1/2 cup shredded onion, divided
1 cup shredded carrots
2 cups shredded celery
1/2 cup chicken broth
2 tablespoons chopped scallions

Marinade
1 tablespoon soy sauce
2 teaspoons dry sherry
2 teaspoons sesame oil
1 tablespoon cornstarch

Seasoning Sauce
2 tablespoons soy sauce
1 tablespoon oyster sauce
1 tablespoon sesame oil
salt and pepper to taste

Method
1. Soak the rice sticks in warm water for 15 minutes or until softened. They will expand to at least twice the volume. Drain thoroughly.

2. Pour the marinade over the pork, toss to mix well and leave to marinate for about 20 minutes.

3. Heat 4 tablespoons of oil over a medium high heat. Sauté half the onion until translucent. Stir-fry the marinated pork until the color changes, stirring constantly to prevent any lumps from forming. Add the carrots and celery, tossing briskly to coat with flavors. Add the seasoning sauce ingredients and continue to stir until well-blended, about 2 minutes. This is the meat sauce you will be using to flavor the rice noodles. Remove to a large bowl and set aside.

4. Wash and clean the wok well; dry with a towel. Heat 4 tablespoons of oil over high heat. Sizzle the rest of the onions for a few seconds and immediately pour in the pre-soaked rice sticks. Turn and toss with two spatulas to coat the rice sticks with hot oil and flavor, about 1 minute. Add the chicken broth and stir-fried pork. Continue stirring and mixing to blend the flavors and to prevent sticking because the liquid evaporates quickly. This takes about 2~3 minutes. When the rice sticks become tender (not mushy) and flavorful, add the chopped scallions and remove to a serving bowl. Serve hot.

8~10 servings

什錦炒飯
Jeweled Fried Rice

In Chinese households, fried rice is often used as a way to consume leftovers. Thus, the best time to make fried rice is after a feast or barbecue picnic since leftover roasted meats or grilled meats are ideal for this dish. Well-cooked fried rice should be aromatic and flavorful, filled with jewels of meat, egg and colorful vegetables. In this recipe, frozen mixed vegetables are used, minimizing the cutting that is normally involved in preparing this dish.

2 cups perfectly cooked rice
   (cold and firm)
oil for stir-frying
2 stalks scallions, chopped,
   white and green parts
   separated
2/3 cup diced Chinese
   sausage or Canadian
   bacon
3 eggs, beaten
1 teaspoon Sha Cha sauce
   (optional)
1 tablespoon light soy sauce
salt and pepper to taste
1 (8-ounce) package frozen
   mixed vegetables

Method

1. Cook the rice at least a few hours in advance whenever possible. Fluff it with a fork while it is still hot.

2. Heat 4 tablespoons of oil over high heat; sizzle about half the white part of the scallions until light brown. Add the sausage, stirring quickly to heat through. Pour in the eggs, turning and mixing to blend with the sausage. Break large pieces of the scrambled eggs into smaller ones. Remove to a plate.

3. Wash the wok thoroughly and dry with a towel. Heat 3 tablespoons of oil over high heat and sizzle the rest of the scallion stems until light brown. Add half the rice, stirring and turning with a spatula (use a Chinese spatula if possible) to coat the grains with the flavored oil, about 1 minute. Add the rest of the rice along with the sha cha sauce, if using, the soy sauce and a dash of salt. Use the back of the spatula to press down on the rice to separate the grains.

4. Return the egg and meat to the wok, then add the mixed vegetables and mix thoroughly with the rice. Add the rest of the scallions as garnish. Remove to a serving bowl and serve hot.

4~6 servings

VEGETABLES : THE CHINESE PASSION

A student once approached me with this question: "I heard the Chinese have wonderful ways with vegetables. Do you have any advice for an American mother trying to raise her child to be a vegetable lover?" I was pleased with her enthusiasm and suggested that she should start exploring Chinese vegetarian products herself. Indeed, the Chinese are known for having the most varied and sophisticated ways of cooking vegetables, but this is not the sole reason why the Chinese are very fond of eating vegetables. The real reason lies in the marvelous variety of Chinese vegetables and vegetarian products that provide a wide range of taste and texture necessary for preparing both simple and elaborate meals.

Producing a tasty meal without using meats can be a difficult task for the novice, but not for a skillful vegetarian chef. Besides using herbs and seasonings to flavor a vegetarian dish, an experienced vegetarian chef also uses aromatic vegetables (fresh, dried and pickled) to bring out the natural taste of fresh vegetables. To find these eateries where only vegetarian meals are served, you must go to the Chinatown in large cities such as New York, San Francisco and Los Angeles. Some Buddhist temples also offer delectable vegetarian meals to visitors on certain days — normally the first and fifteenth day of the Chinese calendar month. Regrettably, not many Chinese restaurants serve a large variety of vegetables to satisfy vegetable lovers. It is the Chinese home cooks who have the greatest repertoire of meatless dishes and this is the reason why home cooking has become such a valued part of Chinese cuisine.

The Chinese are as attached to their native vegetables as Americans are to tomatoes and potatoes. Even when living abroad, the Chinese will go out of their way to find Chinese greens. If Chinese vegetables are unavailable in the stores, the backyard vegetable garden is sometimes the solution. The new demand for Chinese vegetables seems to have had a positive impact on eating habits in this country. The increased presence of Chinese vegetables in supermarkets is a delight to shoppers. Many American vegetable lovers have joined the Chinese to shop at Chinese markets and to grow Chinese vegetables in their backyards.

Although the Chinese love vegetables and eat a great variety of greens, they can't be considered vegetarians in the strict sense, like the monks and nuns in Buddhist temples who are vegetarians because of religious reasons, or like Westerners who adopt a strict vegetarian diet for health reasons. The ideal way to cook vegetables, by Chinese standards, is to cook them with meats. After absorbing the rich taste from meats, the cooked vegetables become extremely tasty and they disappear faster than the meats in a dish. Now you can see why well-cooked vegetables are such valued foods on a Chinese dinner table and why meats are less important in the Chinese diet. Because they know how to flavor vegetables with meats, sauces and spices, Chinese-style vegetables are never boring.

Chinese home cooks are very adventurous in seeking out new additions to their vegetable repertoire. Nothing with good taste is left out, be it domestic or exotic. Naturally, most of the common American vegetables are on the daily menu. A brief glance at how Chinese home cooks treat the common produce will probably give you ideas for cooking some of your favorite vegetables.

Bell Peppers
These are extremely

versatile in Chinese cooking. They are used for flavoring and color contrast in stir-fried dishes. Sometimes they are treated like a seasoning herb when used together with garlic and fermented black beans to flavor spareribs, beef, chicken and seafood. If you can tolerate a little hotness, adding 1 or 2 small green chili peppers will make the flavor go further (if you don't want it too hot, do not use the seeds, which are the hottest part).

Broccoli

Broccoli is great for stir-frying. Whether stirred alone or with meat slices, the taste is marvelous. When cooking to entertain, boil broccoli florets with chicken broth briefly, then use as an edible garnish. Do not throw away the stems; remove the tough outer skin and use the tender-crisp part in salads. Broccoli stems taste best after being marinated with pickle juice or salad dressing.

Cabbage

American cabbage is excellent for Chinese pickles because of its crunchy texture. Many people find it too bland for stir-frying. However, here are some ways to compensate for its uninteresting taste:
* Cut the cabbage into shreds, massage lightly with salt, squeeze out the water and stir-fry over high heat with garlic, chili bean paste and other spices.

* Cut into small squares and stir-fry with pork slices, fermented black beans and oyster sauce.

Carrots

Carrots are great as a decorative vegetable in Chinese cooking. They are used widely in stir-fried and salad dishes (also in dumpling fillings). When stir-frying carrots with other tender vegetables (such as celery or snow peas) always add the carrots first as they take longer to cook. When used in Chinese salads, carrots should be marinated with salt and vinegar for a few minutes to bring out better taste and texture. Carrots taste best when cut into slices (diagonally) or sticks and pickled in a sweet and sour brine (water, sugar, vinegar, salt). Pickled carrots may be used as a garnish or even as a snack.

Cucumbers

Cucumbers play an important role in Chinese cold dishes. Kirby cucumbers are the closest to the delicate Chinese cucumbers in taste and texture; hence they are used extensively in Chinese pickles, relishes, salads and stir-fried dishes. Large cucumbers, being less popular in cold dishes, are used mainly in soups to add a refreshing taste. The popular spices and dressing for cucumbers are Sichuan peppercorns, garlic, sesame oil, chili bean paste, vinegar,

sugar and fermented black beans (for stir-fry only).

Green Beans

Well-cooked Chinese-style green beans taste marvelous. Green beans cannot absorb flavors at all when they are raw. Therefore, they have to be slightly cooked — either by blanching, sautéing or stir-frying — before they are ready to absorb the flavors of seasonings such as garlic, ginger, soy sauce, or marinated meats.

Potatoes

The only time you see potatoes in a Chinese restaurant is when they are served in the fried seafood basket. In Chinese homes, this root vegetable is often used in red-cooked and braised dishes, or in soups to absorb the meat sauce. Some home cooks use shredded potatoes in tossed salad or egg roll filling with satisfying results.

Tomatoes

Because of their high water content, tomatoes do not go well with many stir-fried dishes. However, tomatoes have many uses in Chinese home cooking. They make excellent sauces (sweet-and-sour sauce, or hot-and-sour sauce) for beef, tofu and seafood dishes. They also go well with eggs in stir-fried and soup dishes. The bright red color also makes it a beautiful garnish for many cold platters.

蕃茄炒蛋

Stir-Fried Tomatoes with Eggs

Quick to prepare and flavorful, this is a delicious and soothing everyday dish in Chinese households. Eggs and tomatoes make a perfect pair in terms of color contrast and taste.

oil for stir-frying
1 tablespoon chopped scallions, white and green parts separated
1 large tomato, cut into cubes
2 teaspoons oyster sauce
salt to taste
5 large eggs, beaten

Method

1. Heat 1 tablespoon of oil. Sizzle a few pieces of the white part of the scallions until light brown. Add the tomato cubes, oyster sauce and a dash of salt. Continue stirring until the tomato cubes are soft. Remove and set aside.
2. Wash the wok and dry well. Add a dash of salt and the rest of the scallions (save 2 or 3 stems for sizzling) to the eggs.
3. Heat 5 tablespoon of oil until very hot. Sizzle 2~3 pieces of scallion stems for 5 seconds; immediately pour in the egg mixture. Let it bubble for a few seconds then stir lightly to allow the eggs to set slowly. When the eggs are almost set, add the cooked tomatoes and stir to mix together. Remove and serve hot.

2~4 servings

炒豆芽

Stir-Fried Bean Sprouts

Inexperienced cooks are often perplexed when it comes to cooking a tasty dish of bean sprouts without meat. The answer is fairly simple: First, insist on buying fresh shiny and plump white sprouts. Second, use fragrant herbs or spices to bring out the natural goodness of the sprouts. In this recipe, Sichuan peppercorns and scallions are excellent flavor boosters for the bland sprouts.

1 pound fresh bean sprouts
1 large stalk scallions
oil for stir-frying
1 teaspoon Sichuan
    peppercorns

Seasoning Sauce
1 tablespoon oyster sauce
1 teaspoon vinegar
1 teaspoon sugar
salt and pepper to taste
oil for stir-frying

Method
1. Rinse the bean sprouts lightly. Place in a strainer for 10~15 minutes to drain the water completely. If pressed for time, remove the water with paper towels. This step is crucial to the success of the dish since bean sprouts release a considerable amount of water during cooking. Rinse the scallions lightly and cut into small pieces, with the white and green parts separated.

2. Heat 3~4 tablespoons of oil over high heat. Sauté Sichuan peppercorns until their color begin to change. Turn off the heat and remove the peppercorns from the oil with a Chinese spatula or a slotted spoon. Discard the peppercorns.

3. Reheat the oil until very hot. Sizzle the white part of the scallions until light brown. Immediately add the bean sprouts, stirring constantly while adding the seasoning sauce. Cook for 2 minutes or until the sprouts are well coated with flavor. Add the green part of the scallions for color contrast and extra flavor. Remove to a serving plate. Serve hot or cold.

2~4 servings

青花菜炒蝦
Stir-Fried Broccoli with Shrimp

Broccoli has all the good qualities (color, shape, texture and taste) for an elegant stir-fried dish. It is small wonder that it has become the most welcomed American vegetable in Chinese homes and restaurants. Although parboiling broccoli before stir-frying can shorten the cooking time, you can skip this step by stir-frying the broccoli a little longer. A small amount of fresh shrimp not only enhances the broccoli's flavor but also brings out its color.

1/4 pound fresh shrimp
1 (about 1 pound) head
  broccoli
oil for stir-frying
2 large cloves garlic,
  crushed
2 slices ginger

Marinade
2 teaspoons dry sherry
salt and pepper to taste
1 teaspoon cornstarch

Seasonings
1 tablespoon oyster sauce
1 teaspoon sesame oil
salt to taste

Method
1. Peel, devein and clean
   the shrimp. Drain well.
   Mix with the marinade
   and set aside. Peel the
   fibrous outer skin of the
   broccoli stems with a
   knife. Cut and separate
   the florets. Stems may be
   saved for salads or
   pickles.

2. Blanch the broccoli for 1
   minute in boiling water,
   to which 1 teaspoon of
   salt has been added (as a
   color preserver). Remove
   and immerse in cold
   water. Drain thoroughly.

3. Heat 1 1/2 tablespoons of
   oil over medium heat.
   Stir-fry the shrimp until
   color changes and remove
   immediately. Wash and
   dry the wok. Heat about
2 tablespoons of oil over
high heat. Sauté the
garlic and ginger until
light brown. Add the
broccoli, stirring briskly
to mix with the flavored
oil. Add the seasonings
and continue to stir for 2
minutes. Return the
shrimp to the wok and
toss to mix. Cook for
another minute for
flavors to blend. Remove
to a serving platter.
Carefully arrange the
shrimp on top of the
broccoli so that the two
colors will contrast nicely.
Serve hot.

4 servings

乾扁四季豆
Dry Cooked Sichuan Green Beans

This is the most delicious way to cook green beans, although it might be a little too elaborate for some people. Here the mixed flavors of meat, dried shrimp and the aromatics have a dramatic effect on the green beans, elevating them from the ordinary into something sublime. Sichuan cuisine is noted for its rich and hot taste. This recipe, however, has been slightly modified to suit average tastes. With or without hot pepper, this is a splendid dish.

1 1/2 pounds green beans
1 tablespoon dried shrimp
1/2 cup ground pork
3/4 cup oil for frying
2 tablespoons chopped
   Sichuan mustard green

Marinade

1 teaspoon soy sauce
1/2 teaspoon dry sherry
1 teaspoon cornstarch

Seasonings

2 tablespoons minced garlic
1 teaspoon minced ginger
2 tablespoons minced
   scallions
1 tablespoon light soy sauce
2 teaspoons sugar

Method

1. Snap off the ends of the green beans, rinse lightly and drain. Pat dry with a paper towel. Soak the dried shrimp for 10 minutes in cold water, drain and chop finely. Mix the pork with the marinade and set aside.

2. Heat 3/4 cup of oil over high heat and shallow-fry green beans until they begin to wrinkle (do it in 3 batches for better results). Remove with a slotted spoon and absorb excess oil with paper towels.

3. Pour off all but 1 1/2 tablespoons oil. Turn heat to high, stir-fry the pork and dried shrimp until aromatic and darker in color. Add the pickled mustard green, mixing well with the pork. Return the green beans to the wok and add all the seasonings. Continue tossing and mixing to coat with flavor. This takes 2~3 minutes. Remove to a serving platter. Serve hot or cold.

4~6 servings

回鍋洋芋
Double-Cooked Potatoes

My students call this dish "flavored French fries" since it describes precisely the way it is cooked. I prefer a Chinese-sounding name because this recipe follows the traditional Chinese method of cooking meats. The beauty of this dish lies in its simplicity and luscious taste.

4 large Idaho potatoes, 3~4 inches long
2 tablespoons all-purpose flour
1/2 cup oil for deep-frying
1 1/2 tablespoons chopped scallions

Seasoning Sauce

3/4 cup water or chicken broth
1 teaspoon light soy sauce
1 tablespoon sugar

Method

1. Pick potatoes that are slender in shape. Peel the potatoes and cut into 1/6-inch thick slices. Sprinkle flour over the potatoes and mix lightly.

2. Heat oil over high heat. Deep-fry the potato slices in small batches until golden brown. Remove with a slotted spoon and absorb excess oil with paper towels.

3. Pour out all but 2 tablespoons of oil. Reheat oil over medium-high heat. Sauté a few pieces of scallion stems until light brown. Return potatoes to the wok. Add the seasoning sauce ingredients and simmer for 3~5 minutes over medium-low heat. Potatoes should be tender but not mushy. When the sauce has been reduced to about 1/4 cup, it is done. Garnish with remaining scallions for added flavor. Remove to a serving platter and serve hot.

4 servings

炸菜餅
Vegetarian Gold Coins

I came across this recipe more than a decade ago. Despite the countless times it has been served to guests, it is still an object of admiration on many occasions. This is not a quick recipe to prepare, but once you have tasted it, you will not mind spending 40 to 60 minutes in making it. During my entertaining months, I always make dozens of these heavenly fries and freeze them in individual bags.

1 cup grated potatoes or
 Chinese taro (sold in
 Chinese stores)
1 cup chopped celery
1 cup chopped onion
1 cup grated carrots
1 large egg, beaten
1 cup all-purpose flour
oil for deep-frying

Seasonings
1 tablespoon sesame oil
1 teaspoon salt
1/2 to 2/3 cup sugar

Batter
1 egg, beaten
1/2 cup water or less
 (depending on the water
 content of the vegetables
 added)
1/2 cup flour
1 teaspoon sesame oil

Method
1. Squeeze out excess water
 from the vegetables. In a
 large mixing bowl,
 combine the potatoes,
 celery, onion and carrots
 together with the egg,
 flour and seasonings. Mix
 well until the mixture is
 soft and smooth, adding
 more flour if needed.

2. Preheat the oven to 350°F.
 Line a large cookie sheet
 with aluminum foil. Using
 a spoon and your fingers,
 shape the vegetable
 mixture into balls the size
 of a large cherry and drop
 them onto the cookie sheet.
 Bake at 350°F for 20~25
 minutes or until firm. The
 balls will flatten into the
 shape of coins. Allow the

vegetable coins to cool
slightly. Using your
fingers, coat each piece
with the batter and set
aside.

3. Heat 2 cups of oil over
 high heat. Deep-fry the
 batter-coated vegetable
 coins in small batches
 until both sides turn
 golden brown. Drain well
 and serve immediately.
 Leftovers may be reheated
 in the oven. For best
 results, deep-fry the
 portion you plan to use for
 the day and store the rest
 in the freezer for future
 use.

Makes 25~30 pieces

什錦素燴

Braised Assorted Vegetables

Unless you shop in a Chinese market, you will never find these marvelous vegetarian delicacies — baby soybeans and frozen tender bamboo shoots. They taste so good by themselves that they need just a touch of flavoring, mainly chicken broth and oyster sauce, which gives them a superb taste. If bamboo shoots are unavailable, substitute asparagus.

1/2 pound frozen baby
    soybeans
1/2 cup canned (or fresh)
    straw mushrooms
1 small carrot
2 large pieces frozen bamboo
    shoots
1 small green chili pepper
oil for stir-frying
1 tablespoon chopped garlic,
    divided
1 tablespoon chopped ginger,
    divided
salt and pepper to taste

Seasoning Sauce
1 cup vegetable stock or
    chicken broth
1 tablespoon oyster sauce
1 tablespoon soy sauce
1 teaspoon sugar

Cornstarch Mixture
1 tablespoon cornstarch
2 tablespoons water

Method
1. Bring the frozen baby soybeans to room temperature, rinse and drain thoroughly. Rinse and wash the straw mushrooms well; cut into small pieces about the size of the soybeans. Rinse and peel the carrot and cut into fine pieces. Cut the bamboo shoots and green bell pepper into pieces about the size of the soybeans.

2. Heat 4 tablespoons of oil over high heat and sauté half the garlic and ginger until light brown. Add the soybeans and bamboo shoots. Sprinkle salt to taste, tossing briskly to coat with hot oil. Cook for about 2 minutes. Remove.

3. Clean the wok well and heat 4 tablespoons of oil over high-heat. Sauté the rest of the garlic and ginger until light brown. Add the carrot, tossing for about 1 minute. Add the straw mushrooms and green bell pepper; sprinkle salt and pepper to taste and continue tossing to mix with flavor. Return the baby soybeans and bamboo shoots to the wok; add the seasoning sauce and simmer over medium heat for about 3 minutes. Before removing, add the cornstarch mixture to thicken the sauce. Serve hot.

4~6 servings

素炒粉絲
Stir-Fried Cellophane Noodles

This transparent noodle looks like angel hair but is actually made from mung bean starch, and therefore, can be treated like a vegetable. These noodles are so versatile that there are endless ways in which they can be used. By stir-frying this bean noodle with a variety of colorful vegetables, you can easily concoct an elegant vegetarian home dish in minutes. If you are a meat lover, then by all means, add a batch of meat to enhance the flavor. This is an absolutely glorious dish that can be used as an entrée as well as a side dish.

1 1.7-ounce package
     cellophane noodles
     (preferably Lung-
     Kow brand)
6 dried Chinese mushrooms
4 leaves napa cabbage
1 orange or yellow bell
     pepper
10 snow peas
oil for stir-frying
1/2 teaspoon chopped ginger,
     divided
1 tablespoon chopped garlic,
     divided
1 tablespoon chopped
     scallions or cilantro
salt and pepper to taste

Seasoning Sauce
1/2 cup chicken broth
2 teaspoons soy sauce or fish
     sauce
1 teaspoon sugar

Method
1. Place the cellophane
   noodles, with the string
   intact, in a bowl and fill
   with cold water to cover. In
   a few minutes the noodles
   will become soft and ready
   to use. Before removing
   the string, cut the bundle
   into 2~3 sections for ease
   of handling. Place the
   loose cellophane noodles in
   a strainer to drain
   thoroughly

2. Rinse the dried
   mushrooms lightly and
   soak in 1 cup of warm
   water until soft, 20~30
   minutes. Drain the
   mushrooms, but reserve
   1/2 cup of the soaking
   liquid. Mix the reserved
   soaking liquid with the
   seasoning sauce. Cut the
   mushrooms into thin
   strips.

3. Rinse the napa cabbage
   lightly and drain well. Use
   only the stems. Cut off the
   top section of the leaves
   and save them for soup.
   Cut the stems into thin
   strips. Cut the bell pepper
   into strips. Rinse the snow
   peas, snap off the strings,
   then cut into strips.

4. Heat 2 tablespoons of oil
   over high heat. Sauté half
   the chopped ginger and
   garlic until light brown.
   Add the cabbage, toss
   quickly to coat with oil and
   continue stirring for about
   2 minutes. Sprinkle some
   salt and pepper to taste.
   Pour in about 1/3 of the
   seasoning sauce and add
   the snow peas. Mix well,
   cook for another minute
   and remove.

5. Rinse and dry the wok,
   heat 3 tablespoons of oil
   over high heat. Sauté the
   remaining ginger and
   garlic until light brown.
   Add the cellophane noodles
   and mushrooms, tossing
   quickly to mix with hot oil.
   Immediately pour in the
   remaining seasoning sauce
   for flavoring, mixing
   constantly to separate the
   strands of cellophane
   noodles. Cook for about 2
   minutes, then add the
   cabbage and snow peas.
   Before removing, add the
   scallions and mix the
   colors and flavors together.
   Serve hot or cold.

4 servings

炸茄子
Fried Eggplant

Eggplant has the reputation of being too bland. My son would not eat eggplant unless it was coated with batter and then deep-fried. I've adapted this recipe from the classic "deep-fried stuffed eggplants." They are so tender inside and crispy and flavorful on the outside that one can forget the meat filling and still enjoy the dish. Since they reheat well in the oven, you can make them hours or a day in advance.

2 thin eggplants (purple
　Chinese eggplants
　preferred)
oil for deep-frying

Batter
3/4 cup Bisquick mix
3/4 cup flour
1/3 cup sugar
3/4 cup water (approximate)
1 tablespoon chopped
　scallions
1 tablespoon corn oil
1 teaspoon sesame oil

Method

1. Cut the eggplants diagonally into thin slices the thickness of a biscuit. Mix the batter ingredients to a slightly runny consistency. Dip each slice of eggplant in batter, making sure that each piece is well coated. Place the batter-coated pieces on a cutting board

2. Heat the oil until very hot. Test the temperature by dropping a tiny piece of onion in the oil. If the onion sizzles, the oil is ready for deep-frying. Gently put in the coated eggplants one at a time and fry until both sides turn golden brown. Deep-fry in small batches to avoid crowding.

3. Remove and drain over a wok rack or strainer. Absorb excess oil with paper towels. Serve immediately.

4~6 servings

彩色蛋
Rainbow Egg Custard

This is a very attractive dish that can be easily put together. You can add any colorful vegetables of your choice, but choose those that contrast nicely in colors and withstand long cooking. When using the dish for entertaining, be sure to cut the egg custard into neat-looking pieces and garnish with pretty vegetables.

1/4 medium red bell pepper
1 small carrot
3~4 black olives or Chinese
   mushrooms
1 1/2 cups chicken broth
6 eggs, beaten
2 tablespoons green peas
2 tablespoons chopped ham
   (optional)

Seasonings
salt and pepper to taste
1 teaspoon sesame oil
1 tablespoon chopped
   scallions

Garnish
broccoli, cut into florets,
   blanched

Method
1. Cut the red bell pepper, carrot and black olives into small cubes. Put into a small pot and pour in the chicken broth. Cook over medium-high for about 3 minutes until the vegetables are soft and have absorbed the flavor of the chicken broth. Turn off the heat and let cool slightly. Stir in the seasonings.

2. Line a medium-sized heatproof dish with aluminum foil (it is easier to lift out the cooked custard when a lining is used). Pour in the eggs along with the vegetables and chicken broth. In a large soup pot or a wok, add 2 cups of water and bring to a boil over high heat. Set the container with the egg mixture in the boiling water. Cover and turn down the heat to medium to maintain a gentle boil. Steam for about 20 minutes or until the egg custard is firm. Let cool completely before cutting.

3. Cut the cooled egg custard into 2 to 3-inch blocks and arrange neatly on a serving platter. For a colorful touch, garnish with the blanched broccoli florets.

4 servings

TOFU: THE WONDER FOOD

Tofu, a food that is high in nutrients and yet free of cholesterol, has come a long way toward acceptance in the Western world as the ideal food for healthy diets. Though it may be a popular item in the health food community and has become a regular vegetarian product in supermarkets, tofu, nonetheless, remains a novelty to many Westerners. Perhaps it is time for the original tofu users—the Chinese — to reveal the interesting story of tofu to the world.

According to documented historical records, tofu was invented by Prince Huai Nan of the Han Dynasty (200 B.C.). The invention of tofu was believed to have been an accident, one that might seem amusing to the modern world. Nevertheless, tofu lovers today should be thankful to Prince Huai Nan who, in his quest for immortality, had hired some monks to concoct an elixir from herbs. Unfortunately for Prince Huai Nan, the "elixir" did not work, but the monks had created something better — tofu, a vegetarian product that has become a time-honored food in Asia for centuries.

To Asians, tofu remains a popular food not just because it is healthful, but prepared in the right way, it is considered tasty. Of course, tofu does not have the exciting taste of Peking Duck or fried chicken, but with a soft and soothing texture, tofu has the kind of lasting appeal that is well suited for the everyday diet. Tofu may be equated to potato, the comfort food you seldom become tired of. Believe it or not, a well-prepared tofu dish can be fit for a king. The following anecdote, which has amused many Chinese tofu users, will help explain the unique place of tofu in Chinese cuisine.

Emperor Qian Lung of the Qing Dynasty (1711—1799), a great epicure of his time, often toured the country in plain clothes and one of his pleasures was to explore good food that was unknown to him. The Emperor had never tasted tofu before since this was peasant food and considered too lowly for the royal family. As it happened, one day His Majesty was invited to dine in a peasant's house and there he immediately fell in love with tofu, a very intriguing dish that has a slight taste of meat, yet is lighter and more soothing. The host was a wonderful chef who had cooked tofu to a level of perfection that thoroughly delighted the honored guest. So the Emperor granted his host a handsome reward and happily added tofu to his palace menu.

To those who have never tasted tofu before, it sounds almost incredible that a piece of very bland food could be turned into something you can truly call "tasty." To make it easier to explain, perhaps I could use an analogy: many of us think that lemon desserts are tasty, but we would rarely enjoy the taste of a raw lemon. You must add other ingredients and use special techniques to turn the sour fruit into a piece of tasty cake. The same applies to tofu. By itself, tofu is tasteless; however, if you know how to make a rich aromatic sauce, tofu will soak up all the goodness and be transformed into something very comforting and satisfying. Thus, blandness is not a flaw, but rather an asset that allows tofu to absorb flavors easily, thereby making tofu the most versatile vegetarian food product in Chinese diet. In home cooking, we like to use finely cut pork or beef to lend its rich taste to tofu. Tofu, when paired with seafood such as shrimp, fish, scallops or clam is particularly tasty since seafood sauce can give tofu a more subtle and delicate taste.

A common complaint from Westerners about tofu has always been about its fragility, especially the soft tofu. "How do I keep tofu from falling apart?" was the question my American friends and students often asked me. My answer is that, in most cases, tofu will break into pieces during cooking, so don't think you have made a mistake when that happens. As long as your tofu dish tastes good, you have done a nice job. A simple way to prevent soft tofu from disintegrating easily is to sprinkle some salt all over tofu and allow it to sit for an hour; alternatively you can steam tofu briefly. Salting and steaming firm up the tofu slightly by drawing out excess water. Personally, I use soft tofu more often than firm tofu because soft tofu is easier to season and also cooks faster.

As a tofu user for many decades, I think it is a pity that because of the limited knowledge and exposure people have about tofu, the public (especially the new tofu users) can only identify tofu with the more familiar form — cake tofu. People in this country seem to be totally unaware that there are so many other tofu varieties that are far more interesting than the bland cake tofu. Tofu, just like cheese, comes in various shapes and flavors. These varieties include pressed tofu, fried tofu, shredded tofu, tofu skin and so forth. I find the firmer tofu varieties easier to handle and to flavor than the more fragile cake tofu. If you are cooking tofu for the first time, I suggest that you visit a well-stocked Chinese market and ask for the tofu varieties that will be more likely to bring you happy results.

One special type of tofu that I highly recommend is the brown pressed tofu that comes in square pieces. This is a lightly flavored and semi-dehydrated tofu that has a texture almost like meat. Because of its firm texture, it is easy to cut into any size and shape you desire and is ideal for stir-fries and salads. I have served stir-fried pressed tofu with assorted vegetables and meat to American friends repeatedly and received very positive responses. Everyone was intrigued by the great taste of stir-fried pressed tofu; they thought it was some kind of meat.

Another tofu variety, which has a nice creamy taste and is quite easy to work with, is tofu skin (or tofu stick). Tofu skin comes in frozen and dried forms. Most people prefer the dried tofu stick since it is more versatile and keeps indefinitely. It has a yellowish color and is shaped like a giant hairpin. To use dried tofu sticks properly, soak them in enough water (with 1 tablespoon of baking soda added) to cover and leave overnight or until fully expanded. Then cut into one-inch pieces and cook with chicken broth, soy sauce, aromatics or herbs for 5 to 10 minutes (depending on the brand bought) or until tender and flavorful. The taste is uniquely delicious!

Tofu has been a popular food of the Chinese and Asians for centuries. They enjoy its light taste as well as its health benefits. Tofu appears in many ancient Chinese literary writing. Recently I came across a verse in an article about tofu, which I found most appropriate in describing tofu's attributes. The writer said: "Tofu is as soothing as an old friend, always embracing you with its softness. You never have to worry about its cost and nutrition, nor do you need washing and cleaning. When cooked with flavorful ingredients and good sauce, tofu tastes as marvelous as any other good food." I hope my readers will benefit from this verse and enjoy tofu the way native users do.

炸油豆腐
Double-Cooked Fried Tofu

Like cheese, tofu comes in many forms. This triangular fried tofu has a meaty texture, which makes flavoring a lot easier than the cake tofu. In this unique recipe, it is treated like meat: first marinated overnight, then coated with batter and deep-fried. The result is marvelous, almost like fried dumplings. If desired, you may stuff the tofu with ground meat for a very impressive taste.

1 package brown triangular
    fried tofu (available in
    Chinese markets)
oil for deep-frying

Marinade

2 teaspoons minced scallions
1 teaspoon minced ginger
1 tablespoon soy sauce
1 tablespoon sugar
1 teaspoon sesame oil

Batter

1/2 cup Bisquick
1/2 cup flour
1 cup water
2 teaspoons sesame oil
1 tablespoon sugar
salt and pepper to taste

Method

1. In a medium-sized bowl, pour the marinade over the fried tofu. Blend thoroughly as though marinating meat. Let stand overnight to let the flavors penetrate the tofu.

2. Drain the fried tofu thoroughly. In another bowl, make a smooth batter from the batter ingredients. Dip the tofu into the batter, making sure each piece is well coated. It is preferable to finish coating all the tofu before heating the oil.

Place all the batter-coated tofu on a plate.

3. Heat 2 cups of oil over high heat until hot. Deep-fry the batter-coated tofu until both sides are golden brown. Remove and absorb excess oil with paper towels. Serve immediately.

4~8 servings

蝦仁燴豆腐
Braised Tofu with Shrimp

In Chinese cooking, the matching of tofu with shrimp is considered an ideal marriage. Shrimp cooked in a light sauce make a delicate dressing for tofu. Chopped scallions give extra color and fragrance to the dish. Serve as a main dish along with rice.

2/3 pound shrimp
1/3 pound fresh mushrooms
1 package soft or medium-firm tofu
oil for stir-frying
1/2 tablespoon chopped scallions, white part only
1 tablespoon chopped garlic

Marinade

2 teaspoons dry sherry
2 teaspoons cornstarch
1/2 egg white, beaten
salt to taste

Seasoning Sauce

1/2 can chicken broth
2 tablespoons oyster sauce
1 tablespoon soy sauce
1 teaspoon sugar
salt and pepper to taste

Cornstarch Mixture

2 tablespoons cornstarch
4 tablespoons water
1 teaspoon sesame oil

Garnish

1 tablespoon chopped scallions, green part only

Method

1. Rinse lightly, peel and de-vein the shrimp. Pour the marinade over the shrimp; mix well and set aside. Soak the mushrooms in water and wash off any dirt and grit. Rinse at least twice or until the water runs clear; cut into cubes. Cut the tofu into 1/2-inch cubes and soak in 1 cup of water and 1 teaspoon of salt for 10 minutes; then leave in a strainer to drain.

2. Before cooking, drain shrimp thoroughly (blot excess water with a towel, if necessary). Heat 5 tablespoons of oil over medium-high heat. Sauté half the chopped scallion stems until light brown. Add the shrimp, stirring gently to coat with hot oil. Remove with a slotted spoon as soon as the color changes.

3. Reheat the remaining oil and brown the garlic. Add the mushrooms, tossing constantly until wilted, 2~3 minutes. Add the seasoning sauce and tofu, cover and simmer for 5 minutes.

4. Add the shrimp, toss to mix well and cook for another 2 minutes. Add the cornstarch mixture to thicken the sauce. Garnish with the green part of the scallions. Remove and serve hot.

6 servings

Note

You can use any type of fresh mushrooms available — shitake mushrooms, straw mushrooms, button mushrooms, or oyster mushrooms. Use the canned varieties if fresh mushrooms are not available.

牛肉燴豆腐
Braised Tofu with Beef

Although relatively unknown, this is an extremely delicious dish. Both beef and oyster sauce impart a deep flavor to the bland tofu. The key to success is using soft tofu and a tender cut of beef.

1/2 pound flank steak
1~1 1/2 packages soft tofu
oil for stir-frying
2 stalks scallions, chopped, white and green parts separated
1 tablespoon minced garlic
1/2 cup chicken broth

Marinade
2 teaspoons dry sherry
1 tablespoon soy sauce
2 teaspoons cornstarch
1/2 teaspoon sesame oil

Seasoning Sauce
1 tablespoon soy sauce
2 tablespoons oyster sauce
1 teaspoon chili bean paste (optional)
salt and pepper to taste

Cornstarch Mixture
1 teaspoon sesame oil
2 tablespoons cornstarch
4 tablespoons water

Method

1. Cut the beef into slices (against the grain). Mix well with the marinade and set aside for 30 minutes. Cut the tofu into cubes and soak for 15 minutes in 1 cup of water and 1 teaspoon of salt. Soaking in salt solution makes the tofu firmer. Drain thoroughly with a strainer.

2. Heat 4 tablespoons of oil over high heat and sauté a few pieces of scallions (the white part) until light brown. Add the beef and stir-fry until the red is almost gone. Drain and remove with a slotted spoon. Remove the oil to a small bowl. Clean and dry the wok thoroughly.

3. Return the oil to the wok and add 3 more tablespoons of oil; heat until very hot. Sauté the garlic and white part of the scallions until light brown. Add the seasoning sauce and chicken broth. Bring to a boil then add the tofu. Cover, lower the heat and simmer for 3 minutes. Add the beef and cook for another 2 minutes. Add the cornstarch mixture and the green part of the scallions. Mix well and remove to a serving platter. Serve hot.

4~6 servings

豆乾炒雞絲

Stir-Fried Pressed Tofu with Chicken

Pressed tofu is a favorite food of my family. I use it more often than cake tofu because it is so much easier to cut into strips and is excellent when stir-fried with ingredients that contribute an interesting taste and texture. It is crucial to look for the best brand in the market. On the East Coast, it is Wen's. You may find other equally good brands in your area.

4 squares pressed tofu
1 medium red bell pepper
3 stalks celery
1/3 pound chicken breast, shredded
oil for stir-frying
1 tablespoon minced garlic
1 teaspoon sweet bean sauce or oyster sauce (optional)
1 tablespoon shredded onion
salt and pepper to taste

Marinade for Chicken

1 teaspoon rice wine or dry sherry
1 teaspoon soy sauce
1 teaspoon sesame oil
2 teaspoons cornstarch
salt and pepper to taste

Seasonings for Tofu

1 tablespoon chicken broth
1 teaspoon oyster sauce

Seasonings for Chicken

1 tablespoon chicken broth
1 teaspoon soy sauce
1 teaspoon oyster sauce

Method

1. Rinse tofu lightly and cut into slices. Stack 4 slices each time and cut into thin strips. Rinse the bell pepper and celery separately and cut into strips. Marinate the shredded chicken briefly and set aside.

2. Heat 2 tablespoons of oil over high heat until very hot. Sizzle the garlic briefly. Add the bell pepper, tossing quickly to heat through and to coat with hot oil, about 1 minute. Add the tofu strips and continue to stir while adding the chicken broth, oyster sauce, and some salt and pepper to taste. Cook for another 2~3 minutes. Just before turning off the heat, add the celery. Mix well and remove. Clean and dry the wok well.

3. Add 1 teaspoon of sweet bean paste, if available, to the marinated chicken. Heat 2~3 tablespoons of oil over high heat. Sizzle the onion until light brown. Add the marinated chicken and cook until color changes, turning quickly to separate the shreds and to coat with hot oil. Return the cooked tofu and vegetables to the wok. Add the chicken broth, soy sauce and oyster sauce. Gently toss to let the tofu absorb flavors from both the chicken and vegetables. Cook for about 2 minutes, then remove to a serving platter. Serve hot or cold.

6 servings

Note

Peel the outer fibrous strings of celery for a crisp-tender texture — by Chinese standards, this means cooking vegetables until they are still crisp, yet barely tender. If available, use Chinese celery, which has a more pungent taste.

蘭花豆干
Fragrant Tofu Snack

One of my relatives from mainland China gave me this recipe. After some improvisation and a few tests, it became popular among family members and friends. The beauty of this dish is that it has the chewy subtle taste of meat, yet contains only vegetarian protein and nutrients. This could well be an excellent meat substitute for vegetarian fans.

1 pound brown pressed tofu
2 cups oil for frying

Seasoning Sauce

2 cups chicken broth
2 star anise
2 teaspoons chili paste (optional)
1 tablespoon oyster sauce
2 tablespoons soy sauce
2 tablespoons sugar
pepper to taste
2 stalks scallions, or 1 small onion, cut into large pieces
4 cloves garlic, slightly crushed

Method

1. Look for the best brand of pressed tofu, one with a light brown color and softer texture. For best results, you need to cut both sides of the tofu in a special way. Rinse and drain the tofu; dry well. Using a kitchen knife, make 8~10 equally spaced cuts about 1/3 through the thickness of the tofu, starting the first cut parallel to one edge. Flip the tofu over. Beginning from one corner, make 10~12 diagonal cuts of the same spacing and depth as the other side. This unique cutting method exposes the interior surface of the tofu to the heat and sauce, making it easier for the tofu to absorb flavors. When you see zipper-like cuts on the small sides of the tofu, you know you have done a nice job.

2. Heat the oil over medium high heat and deep-fry the tofu until both sides are light golden brown, 5~8 minutes. When the tofu pieces become firmer and the cracks begin to open, it is done. Remove and drain on the racks.

3. Transfer the fried tofu to a medium-sized soup pot, add the seasoning sauce and cook over medium heat for 20~30 minutes. Turn the heat off and let the tofu soak in the sauce for a while before serving. Cut each cooked tofu into 4 pieces on the diagonal and set on an attractive serving plate with some green garnish. Serve cold.

6~8 servings

CHINESE SALADS: The Gem of Chinese Home Cooking

Contrary to the image created by Chinese restaurants, stir-frying is not the only method that the Chinese use for cooking vegetables. They are, in fact, masters of pickles and vegetable preserves, which have become the delight of the Chinese gourmet.

As a child, my favorite snack was a tantalizing array of pickled salads purchased on the street in China from a pushcart vendor. My craving for marinated vegetables has continued into my adult life. Whenever I go to a special eatery or attend a home party, I would often be inclined to look for the best tasting vegetable dishes to add to my repertoire. And I have been fortunate enough to find many interesting recipes, a few of which I have included in this chapter.

Although pickled salads are very popular in the Chinese home, freshly made pickled salads are seldom found in the stores. When I introduce them to my guests, I always receive compliments, which delights me for days.

Making a tasty Chinese marinated salad is very simple. In the recipes that follow you will discover that the key to flavoring raw vegetables is salting. The salting process is very simple — cut the vegetables into bite-size pieces, massage liberally with salt and then rinse thoroughly to remove all the salt. After salting, the vegetables are literally half "cooked." This is the best stage for them to absorb the combined flavors of seasonings. With a touch of imagination, you can make the taste of your salad surprisingly interesting.

Here are some basic techniques that will surely bring happy results to your Chinese salads:

Pickled Salads

Root vegetables such as carrots, red radishes and daikons are cut into smaller pieces and marinated in an aromatic sour brine for a number of days until they become flavorful and crunchy. These pickled vegetables are extremely palatable once they lose the sharpness and unpleasant raw taste. If you don't know how to make the brine, buy a large jar of ready-made pickles (medium-sour) from the stores. After finishing the pickles, throw pieces of cut carrots and red radishes into the brine; within three days you will have a jar of delicious Chinese-style pickles.

Hot Assembled Salads

Crunchy vegetables such as cabbage and Kirby cucumbers are cut into strips and stir-fried briefly (2 ~ 3 minutes.) During this time various seasonings are added. After the dish has cooled, it is then refrigerated for a few hours for thorough flavor penetration and extra crispiness. Salads assembled this way taste as irresistible and pleasantly crunchy as pickled salads, but is done within a day.

Cold Tossed Salads

Hard vegetables such as daikon or carrots are first shredded and then salted to draw out the water and to temper the sharp taste. Salting plays a vital part here. It gives the vegetables instant crispiness and prepares them for quick flavor penetration. After salting and rinsing, dressings are added. Chinese salad dressings are simple combinations with "sweet-and-sour," "hot-and-sour," or "hot-and-aromatic" tastes. Dressing ingredients are usually selected from the following seasonings and spices: sesame oil, soy sauce, vinegar, sugar, chili bean paste, hot oil, Sichuan peppercorn oil, ginger, garlic, scallions and cilantro.

麻辣黄瓜
Sichuan Cucumber Salad

This zesty summer dish is so popular that it is well liked by Chinese in most regions. The cucumbers are first salted and then marinated with a very robust dressing. It becomes crunchy and flavorful within just hours or overnight.

8 Kirby cucumbers (pickling
   cucumbers) or Chinese
   cucumbers
2 teaspoons salt
oil for stir-frying
2 teaspoons Sichuan
   peppercorns (optional)

Seasoning Sauce

2 teaspoons fermented black
   bean chili sauce
2 tablespoons vinegar
1 teaspoon salt
2 tablespoons soy sauce
3 tablespoons sugar
2 tablespoons sesame oil
3 tablespoons minced garlic

Method

1. Rinse the cucumbers and
   cut away any blemished
   parts. Cut into 1 1/2-inch
   pieces and place in a
   mixing bowl. Add 2
   teaspoons of salt to the
   cucumbers and massage
   lightly with one hand for
   about a minute. Then rinse
   under running water and
   drain thoroughly.

2. Heat 3 tablespoons of oil.
   Sauté the Sichuan
   peppercorns until the color
   changes. Turn off the heat
   and discard the

peppercorns with a slotted
spoon. Immediately pour
the seasoning sauce and
cucumbers into the
flavored oil. With the heat
turned off, stir thoroughly
until well blended.

3. Remove and refrigerate
   overnight to let the flavor
   mellow slowly. Serve cold.
   This dish keeps at least a
   week in the refrigerator. If
   desired, double the recipe.

   6~8 servings

涼拌茄子

Eggplant Salad

Like green beans, eggplants do not absorb flavors when raw. For best results, tenderize the eggplant first by sautéing or steaming before adding the sauce. The following is a simple light-tasting recipe. If you like a stronger and richer flavor, chili sauce or meat sauce may be added.

3 purple Chinese eggplants
oil for sauteing
1 teaspoon Sichuan
   peppercorns
1 tablespoon coarsely
   chopped garlic
1 tablespoon chopped
   scallions for garnish

Dressing

1 tablespoon soy sauce
1 tablespoon oyster sauce
2 teaspoons sesame oil
2 teaspoons vinegar
2 tablespoons sugar
1/4 teaspoon chili paste
   (optional)

Method

1. Rinse the eggplants and cut into halves lengthwise. Score the back of the eggplants diagonally for heat penetration and eye-appeal. In a pan or wok, heat 3 tablespoons oil over medium-high heat. Lightly sauté both sides of eggplants briefly. Remove before they lose the purple color completely.

2. Heat 2 tablespoons of oil over medium-heat and sauté the peppercorns until the color changes. Turn off the heat and discard the peppercorns with a slotted spoon. Infusing the oil with peppercorns adds a great deal of aroma to the dish.

3. Reheat the oil and add the garlic. Sauté until light brown. Turn off the heat and add the oil and garlic to the dressing. Mix well and pour the flavorful mixture over the sauteed eggplants. Serve warm or cold. Garnish with chopped scallions before serving.

2~4 servings

五彩拌粉絲

Cellophane Noodle Salad

Cellophane noodles have a prominent place in Chinese home cooking. They are used extensively in soups and stir-fried dishes. The bouncy and crunchy texture goes marvelously with crisp vegetables, making it an ideal ingredient for salads. This is a healthy and tasty dish; make it your everyday fare.

2 small packages cellophane
   noodles (Lung Kow brand)
2 large Kirby cucumbers
   (pickling cucumbers)
2 medium carrots
oil for sautéing
1 teaspoon Sichuan
   peppercorns
1/2 package Canadian bacon
   or cooked ham, shredded
   (optional)

Dressing
2 tablespoons minced garlic
2 tablespoons light soy sauce
1 tablespoon sesame oil
2 tablespoons vinegar
2 tablespoons sugar
salt to taste

Method
1. In a saucepan, bring
   approximately 4 cups of
water to a boil. Remove
the pan from the stove and
immerse the cellophane
noodles in the hot water
for 5~10 minutes. By now
the noodles are already
cooked. Drain thoroughly
and cut into shorter
lengths for easy handling.

2. Use a good shredder and
process the cucumbers and
carrots separately (or cut
into thin matchsticks with
a kitchen knife). For
tastier carrots, marinate
them with a pinch of salt
and 1/2 tablespoon each of
vinegar and sugar for at
least 20 minutes. But do
not add salt to the
shredded cucumbers.
Drain well before mixing.

3. Heat 2 tablespoons of oil
and sauté the Sichuan
peppercorns until the color
changes. Turn off the heat.
Discard the peppercorns
and pour the flavored oil
into the dressing.

4. On a large plate, spread
the cellophane noodles
neatly to form a bottom
layer. Then top with
shredded cucumbers and
carrots. Lastly, spread
shredded Canadian bacon
on top to complete this
colorful salad combination.
When ready to serve,
simply pour the dressing
over the entire dish.

6 servings

涼拌青花菜梗

Broccoli Stem Salad

A student in my cooking class told me that she used to throw away the broccoli stems since she did not know what to do with them. I gave her this recipe and she was quite pleased with the result. You, too, can turn the "useless" stems into a delectable salad dish.

4 stalks of broccoli stems (from 2 heads of broccoli)
1 teaspoon salt
2 tablespoons coarsely chopped garlic
1 tablespoon light soy sauce or fish sauce
2 teaspoons vinegar
2 teaspoons sugar
2 teaspoons sesame oil

Method

1. Peel off the tough skin of the broccoli stems. Rinse well and cut into thin slices. Add salt to the broccoli stems and mix with your hand. Salting eliminates the raw taste of the stems. Rinse lightly and drain thoroughly.

2. Combine the garlic, soy sauce, vinegar, sugar and sesame oil and mix well with the broccoli stems. Marinate for at least two hours before serving. Chilling overnight improves the flavor and gives it a crisper texture. A small amount of chili bean paste can be added to boost the flavor.

2~4 servings

廣東泡菜
Cantonese-Style Pickled Salad

This salad was my childhood favorite, an evening snack that I indulged in on street corners in the summertime. A few years back I was amazed to find out how simple it is to make this dish. It takes no more than the cutting of crunchy vegetables and soaking them in sweet-and-sour brine. In addition to its simplicity, this is a surprisingly speedy and tasty recipe that can be done within a day or two. Use it as a side dish or as an edible garnish. For people who love snacking, this may be a healthy substitute for candy.

2 large carrots
1/3 of a small American
    cabbage
1 medium daikon

Pickling Juice
4 slices ginger
1 tablespoon salt
3 cups cold water
1/2 cup cider vinegar
1/2 cup sugar

Method
1. Rinse the carrots, cabbage and daikon separately. Cut the carrots and daikon into slices. Cut the cabbage into 1-inch squares.

2. In a deep bowl (non-reactive) or large jar, mix the ingredients for the pickling juice together. Add the vegetables to the pickling juice. If necessary, add water to cover.

3. For quick results, leave the pickled vegetables out of the refrigerator to marinate for 1~2 days until the raw taste is gone. Then put them in the refrigerator to develop a crunchy texture. You may leave the vegetables in the pickling juice for another few days or so. But try to finish them soon or they will lose their crispness. The pickling juice may be reused.

6~10 servings

拌紅白蘿蔔絲

Carrot and Daikon Salad

Here is a quick and tasty recipe. If you have a good vegetable shredder, you can easily turn out a very interesting dish in just a few minutes. You will find it especially convenient when entertaining guests.

3 medium carrots
1 large daikon
2 teaspoons salt

Dressing
1 teaspoon shredded ginger
3 tablespoons vinegar
3 tablespoons sugar
2 teaspoons sesame oil
1 stalk cilantro, cut into 1/4-
 inch pieces

Method
1. Rinse the carrots and daikon well. Cut into thin strips with a good shredder or a kitchen knife. Combine the two vegetables in a mixing bowl, add salt and mix with your hands. Salting helps to speed up the pickling process.

2. Squeeze out excess water from the salted vegetables. Taste to check the saltiness. Add more salt if too bland or rinse again if too salty.

3. Add the dressing to the salted vegetables and toss to mix well. You can serve immediately or refrigerate for later use. It keeps up to a week in the refrigerator.

4~6 servings

脆拌紫紅包心菜

Crispy Red Cabbage Salad

Plain, stir-fried American red cabbage is often lacking in taste. However, the crisp texture of this cabbage is excellent for salads and pickles. I developed this recipe by combining the techniques of stir-frying and tossing and the end result is marvelous.

1 small head red cabbage
1 teaspoon salt
oil for stir-frying
1/2 tablespoon Sichuan
    peppercorns
6 large cloves garlic, crushed
4 slices ginger
1 large stalk scallion or sprigs
    of cilantro, chopped

Seasonings

1 tablespoon dry sherry
1/2 tablespoon soy sauce
2 tablespoons sugar
2 tablespoons vinegar
2 teaspoons chili paste

Method

1. Rinse the cabbage lightly; cut into shreds and sprinkle salt on it. Massage the cabbage for about 2 minutes until slightly moist. Drain excess water.

2. Heat 5 tablespoons of oil over high heat. Add the Sichuan peppercorns and allow them to sizzle until the color changes. Turn off the heat and use a slotted spoon to discard all the peppercorns. Turn the heat to high and sauté the garlic cloves and ginger until light brown. Pour in the cabbage and stir to mix with the oil. Add the seasonings one at a time and stir continuously. Cook 4~5 minutes until the cabbage wilts slightly and the ingredients are well blended. Add the chopped scallions or cilantro before removing the cabbage from the wok. Cool to room temperature. Serve cold.

6~8 servings

SOUPS:

THE PERFECT ACCOMPAINMENT TO A MEAL

It may come as a surprise that wonton soup is never served as a soup course in traditional Chinese households, but rather as an afternoon or midnight snack. Nor is hot-and-sour soup an everyday fare — it is more often served when entertaining or on special occasions. Despite the incredible variety, there are basically two kinds of home-style soups: the light soup and the heavy soup. You may call the light soup a quick and convenient dish since it can be made effortlessly within minutes with ready stock or chicken broth. You need almost no skill except the good judgment of knowing what goes into the broth to make a pot of soothing, savory soup.

Here are some guidelines for beginners:

Light Soups

Light soups should be smooth and clear since it is intended to accompany the meal as a savory beverage.

Ingredients for light soups should be tender, easy to cook and with contrasting color and texture. Although a great variety of ingredients may be used in light soups, the following ingredients are frequently used by Chinese home cooks: eggs, ham, seafood, shredded or sliced meats, tofu, cellophane noodles, seaweed, corn, tomatoes, napa cabbage and other leafy vegetables. Examples of light soups are egg drop soup, cabbage tofu soup and chicken mushroom soup.

Heavy Soups

Slightly different from light soups, heavy soups are filled with solid meat ingredients (often large pieces) and starchy vegetables and are often thickened with heavy broth (extracts from various food products). This type of soup normally requires long simmering to tenderize the meat and to mellow the flavor. The result is substantial and luscious-tasting soup. Examples of

heavy soups are hot-and-sour soup, seafood casseroles and fire pot. Certainly, to make elaborate soup means extra work. For this reason, most home cooks use quick light soups for daily meals and reserve heavy soups for special occasions or as a body warmer on cold days.

The Key to Good Soups

Obviously, the key to successful soups lies in the stock. Simply adding meats or vegetables with good texture and taste to a pot of flavorful stock will result in delectable soup. There are many ways of making good stock.

Traditionally, a professional Chinese cook brews his stock in a very elaborate and extravagant manner. It takes several chickens plus long hours of simmering just to produce a small pot of stock the traditional way. Fortunately, modern cooks need not follow this formula. I find canned chicken broth extremely convenient and versatile. If I want my soup to have more depth in taste, I simply throw in a few pieces of spareribs or chicken bones. To make the soup even more impressive, I can easily count on Smithfield ham or dried Chinese seafood (dried shrimp, fish, or oysters) to lend their distinctive flavors.

To make your soup from scratch, these guidelines can be helpful:

- Select pork bones, spareribs, chicken bones or chicken feet for the stock. Avoid using bones with a strong taste. Beef and lamb stock do not seem to blend well with other ingredients when used in soups.

- Before making your stock, always rinse out any blood in the bones as it can create impurities. Then immerse bones in boiling water to eliminate any odor.

- Meat bones provide a good amount of natural calcium for the body; however, the grease produced in soups and stocks can be intimidating to health-conscious home cooks.

Here is an easy solution: Refrigerate the fat filled soup. Once it is chilled, all the oil and grease will collect at the top. Just skim off that layer of gelled fat and you can enjoy tasty, grease-free soups with a clear conscience.

- Fresh or dried seafood is a great source of flavor. My secret in creating a delicate stock is to boil a few pieces of dried shrimp or dried squid in half a pot of water to extract the good flavor.

- Even if you do not have ready stock or chicken broth on hand, you can still create delectable soups by using the Chinese quick sautéing method. Heat 1 tablespoon of oil to the smoking point; sizzle a few pieces of ginger, scallion stems or onion until fragrant; immediately add 5 to 6 cups of water, then season with salt, pepper and soy sauce. This is your basic broth for light soups.

蕃茄蛋花湯

Tomato Egg Drop Soup

"Picky" Chinese household members will not be satisfied with just plain egg drop soup. Thus the everyday cook needs to search out some interesting accompaniments that has color and taste, such as tomatoes, corn, or even seafood, to liven up the plain egg drop soup. This is where creativity comes into play in Chinese home cooking.

6 cups water
2 cans chicken broth
2 medium tomatoes, cut
   into chunks or slices
3 eggs, beaten, with a
   dash of salt added
salt to taste
1 tablespoon scallions
1 teaspoon sesame oil

Method

1. Bring the water, chicken broth and tomatoes to a gentle boil. Cook for about 3~5 minutes or until the tomatoes blend into the soup.

2. Hold the bowl containing the eggs about 8 inches above the pot and pour the eggs slowly, in a circular motion, into the soup. This will make the egg drops look beautiful and taste better.

3. Add the salt, scallions and sesame oil; mix well. Transfer to a deep bowl and serve this colorful soup hot.

8~10 servings

排骨冬瓜湯
Spareribs and Winter Melon Soup

Elegant and soothing, this soup is absolutely fabulous. Winter melon absorbs the meat flavor like a sponge, and in turn, lends a marvelous taste to the spareribs. I love the refreshing taste of winter melon — it goes well with almost any kind of clear soup. Try making spareribs and winter melon into a stew dish. It tastes equally delicious.

1 pound spareribs
4 slices ginger
2 tablespoons dry sherry
salt to taste
1 pound winter melon
1 can chicken broth
  (optional)
1 tablespoon chopped
  scallions
1 teaspoon sesame oil

Method

1. Have your butcher cut the spareribs straight across into 3 strips. Then cut the membrane between the ribs to get squares; rinse lightly. Bring 1/2 pot of water to a rolling boil and add the spareribs, ginger and sherry. Lower the heat to medium-high. Remove any impurities that come to the top. Maintain a gentle boil for about 30 minutes with the pot partially covered. Add salt to taste.

2. Cut away the thick skin of the winter melon, then cut the flesh into large wedges. Winter melon cooks in 15~20 minutes, so add to the sparerib soup when the meat is almost tender. If you like the soup to have an even richer flavor, add a can of chicken broth. Before serving, add the scallions and sesame oil. Serve hot.

6~8 servings

Note

Most Chinese markets carry ready-cut packaged winter melon. Look for a clean piece with pale green skin and firm white flesh.

冬菇蘿蔔湯

Daikon Mushroom Soup

I found this recipe in a home-style Chinese restaurant. The delicate taste of this soup has surprised many diners. They found it hard to believe that a little-known vegetable like daikon could produce such high quality taste. Daikon soup is not a new recipe. It was on the emperors' menus centuries ago.

5 medium dried Chinese
   mushrooms
1/2 cup ground pork
1 small daikon (about 1 1/4
   pounds)
2 cans chicken broth
5 cups water

Marinade
1 teaspoon dry sherry
1 tablespoon light soy sauce
1 tablespoon cornstarch

Seasonings
1 teaspoon sesame oil
salt and pepper to taste
1 tablespoon chopped
   cilantro

Method
1. Soak the mushrooms in 1 cup of water until soft. Reserve the soaking liquid, dice the mushrooms and set aside. Mix the ground pork with the marinade and let stand for 3~5 minutes. Cut the daikon into 1/3-inch cubes.

2. In a medium-sized soup pot, boil the chicken broth, water and mushrooms (with the soaking liquid) for 3 minutes or until the flavor of the mushrooms is fully extracted. Add the pork and daikon. Cook until the daikon becomes tender, about 5 minutes. Mix in the seasonings and remove to a soup bowl. Serve hot.

6~8 servings

眉豆湯

Black-Eyed Pea Soup

Black-eyed peas are not only wholesome but also very tasty when cooked in soups. The best accompaniment to black-eyed peas is meat bones. Long simmering draws out all the goodness from the bone marrow, which melts into the creamy pea soup, giving it a rich taste.

2-3 chicken drum sticks or
    pork spareribs
2 tablespoons dry sherry
1 can chicken broth
3 slices ginger
1 cup black-eyed peas
salt to taste
1 tablespoon minced cilantro

Method

1. Cut a slit on each drumstick and marinate with the sherry for 10 minutes.

2. In a medium-sized stockpot, bring half a pot of water and 1 can of chicken broth to a boil. Add the chicken (with the sherry) and ginger; boil for 10 minutes over medium-high heat. Add the black-eyed peas and salt to taste. Cook, with the pot uncovered, for 50~60 minutes or until the soup becomes creamy. Stir occasionally and add water as needed. Garnish with cilantro when the taste is well blended. Remove and serve immediately.

6~8 servings

蛤蜊湯

Clam Soup

This light clam soup has an unique ocean flavor and has become a favorite everyday fare in some Chinese homes. It is vitally important to buy the right kind of clams — the ones which have minimum sand — and you might have to ask around to find the best source. Also bear in mind that clams should never be put in the freezer or they will die and become inedible. Try to buy light-brown-colored clams (such as Maine Mahogany), which are much easier to clean.

1 pound brown clams
4 thin slices ginger
1/4 cup rice wine or dry sherry
1 cup chicken broth
4-5 cups water
salt and pepper to taste
basil or cilantro for garnish

Method

1. Look for clean-looking, brownish clams. Before cooking, soak the clams in water for about 15 minutes to purge the clams of sand. Rinse a few times until water runs clear.

2. In a medium stockpot, add the clams, ginger, rice wine, chicken broth and water. Boil over medium-high heat for about 5 minutes; skim off any impurities that come to the top. Maintain a gentle boil for a few more minutes to allow the flavor to mellow slowly. Add the salt and pepper and turn off the heat. Remove to a soup bowl, garnish with basil or cilantro. Serve immediately.

4~6 servings

豆腐蝦仁湯
Shrimp and Tofu Soup

Soft tofu and shrimp combine wonderfully in braised dishes. They look even more elegant in this clear soup dish. Add a few leaves of bright green Chinese bok choy, and you have a glorious dish for the eyes and for the palate to enjoy.

1/2 pound fresh medium
  shrimp
1/2 teaspoon salt
1 large square soft tofu
few leaves of baby bok choy
2 chicken drumsticks or pork
  spareribs
3 cups chicken broth
1 teaspoon sherry
3 cups water
salt and pepper to taste

Marinade
2 teaspoons dry sherry
2 thin slices ginger
salt and pepper to taste

Method
1. Look for very fresh shrimp that will turn a bright red when cooked. Peel and devein the shrimp. Rinse and drain well. Add the marinade and let sit for about 10 minutes. Drain the shrimp again before cooking. Sprinkle 1/2 teaspoon of salt over the tofu square to draw out some water and firm it up slightly. This will take about 10 minutes. Rinse the bok choy well and cut into 1-inch lengths.

2. To give the tofu a deeper flavor, you need to make a rich broth. In a stockpot, boil the drumsticks or spareribs in chicken broth, sherry and water for 5~10 minutes to extract flavor. Remove the chicken and any impurities from the broth. Pour off excess water from the tofu and cut into small cubes. Add tofu to the broth and cook over medium heat for 3~5 minutes to absorb flavor.

3. Add the shrimp and bok choy to the broth. These cook fairly quickly, about 2 minutes. Once overcooked, the shrimp will toughen up and the bok choy will lose its color and shape. Add salt and pepper to taste before removing to the soup bowl. Serve immediately.

4 servings

酸辣湯
Hot and Sour Soup

Hot and sour soup, with its hearty, stimulating taste and diverse textures, deserves its international fame. There are many versions of this dish. My favorite version contains sea slugs, which may not appeal to Westerners (unless you are a very adventurous diner). But the following version, with a good broth and added tomatoes, has won many hearts. Aside from taste and texture, it has an attractive color.

1/2 pound pork loin
4~6 wood ears
1 cup shredded bamboo shoots
2 tablespoons shredded Sichuan mustard green
1 square soft tofu
1 medium tomato, cut into wedges

Soup Base
1/2 pound spareribs
2 cans chicken broth
6 cups water

Marinade
2 teaspoons dry sherry
1 tablespoon soy sauce
2 teaspoons cornstarch

Seasonings
1 tablespoon light soy sauce
2 teaspoons sesame oil
1 tablespoon cider vinegar
salt and pepper to taste
1 tablespoon chopped scallions

Cornstarch Mixture
1/4 cup cornstarch mixed
1/2 cup water

Method
1. In a large soup pot, bring the soup base to a rolling boil. Reduce the heat to medium-high and maintain a gentle boil for at least 20 minutes.

2. Cut the pork into thin strips and mix with the marinade; set aside. Soak the wood ears in cold water for 15 minutes or until they are soft. Rinse well until free of grit and cut into thin strips. If the bamboo shoots and pickled mustard green are not in shredded form, cut them into thin strips. The soft tofu has the best texture for this recipe. The trick to keep it from falling apart is to sprinkle 1/2 teaspoon salt all over the tofu and let it sit for 10 minutes; then cut it into strips.

3. After 20 minutes of cooking, the soup should taste rich and flavorful. Remove the spareribs and any impurities from the soup. Bring to a boil again, add the tomato and cook for about 5 minutes. Add the pork, stirring constantly to separate the pieces. Add the wood ears, bamboo shoots, mustard green and tofu; cook for another 3 minutes. Stir in the seasonings and mix well. Thicken with the cornstarch mixture and remove to a soup bowl. Serve immediately.

6~8 servings

蘿蔔鴨子湯
Duck and Daikon Soup

Duck has been well publicized for its marvelous taste in roasted and red-cooked dishes. However, many people are unaware that duck also tastes great in soups. In this recipe, the duck imparts a rich taste to the soup, which is similar to that of the famous Chinese ham. And daikon, the humble vegetable, actually enhances the taste of the duck while absorbing some goodness from the broth. This soup is absolutely delicious, fit for any honored guest.

1/2 (2~3 pounds) medium duck
1/2 cup rice wine or dry sherry, divided
4 slices ginger, divided
1 cup chicken broth
1 medium daikon
1 teaspoon chopped cilantro

Method

1. Trim excess fat from the duck, but retain the skin (optional) for eye-appeal. Rinse and drain well, place in a stockpot and add water to cover. Also add half of both the wine and ginger; cook for 10 minutes to eliminate some of the fat. Remove the duck from the pot and let cool slightly. Cut the duck in halves. Save one portion for other uses and cut the other half into 1-inch pieces and set aside. Remove the oily broth to a bowl for future use. Refrigerate the broth until the fat congeals. Lift it off and discard.

2. Return the duck pieces to the pot. Add 5~6 cups of water, the chicken broth (to compensate for partial loss of flavor) and the remaining ginger and wine. Bring to a boil and maintain a gentle boil for about 30 minutes or until the broth deepens in flavor. Rinse and peel the daikon; cut into chunks. Add the daikon chunks to the duck soup and continue to cook for another 30 minutes or until the daikon becomes translucent. Add the chopped cilantro before transferring to a soup bowl. Serve immediately.

4 servings

PORK: THE VERSATILE MEAT

At the mention of pork, the Chinese automatically thinks of juicy flavorful dumplings, tender meatballs, succulent spareribs and aromatic pork shreds. Pork, for many reasons, has an irreplaceable place in Chinese cooking. First of all, pork is the traditional meat of the Chinese kitchen; hence, there is a greater repertoire of pork dishes in the average households. Second, pork has a finer grain and richer taste than beef and lamb. Third, other meats tend to toughen easily during stir-frying, whereas pork remains tender and juicy even when it is slightly overcooked. Last, but not least, pork is extremely versatile in Chinese-style cooking — almost every part can be made into a palatable dish.

In Chinese home cooking, pork is commonly used in the following ways:

Slices and shreds for stir-fried dishes, soups and braised dishes. These are normally cut from pork chops, tenderloin, or the lean part of the shoulder. They are rarely cooked alone but usually paired with other ingredients (mainly vegetables) to enhance flavors. Shredded pork is highly prized by critical Chinese gourmets.

Pork shoulder or pork chunks for red-cooked braising (cooked in soy sauce). These are cuts from the shoulder, fresh ham, or fresh bacon. They are first browned in oil and then simmered slowly in soy sauce and spices until very tender. Although on the fatty side, the marvelous taste of these dishes is unmatched.

Pork chops for deep-frying or barbecuing. These are best liked by children and are used widely for outdoor cookouts and parties. The pork chops are first marinated overnight (or at least six hours) then placed on a grill or deep-fried. Either way, the taste is unbeatable.

Innards (kidneys, tripe, hearts) for stewing or stir-frying. When properly cooked, these innards can be very interesting. But these days it is almost out of fashion to cook innards. Nevertheless, pork tripe is the only offal that is still prepared in home kitchens and some restaurants. This is because pork tripe has a delicate flavor (after special treatment) and an elastic and crunchy texture that fascinate the Chinese; thus, it holds a unique place in many famous recipes.

Spareribs are the most popular cuts in Chinese home cooking. Spareribs are naturally sweet and flavorful. They require only minimum skill and effort to turn into an outstanding dish. This may be the reason why they are such valued cuts in Chinese kitchens. Almost everyone in China loves sweet-and-sour spareribs or steamed black bean spareribs. I have included these recipes for two reasons: First, they are relatively easy to prepare and are more likely to bring success on your first try. Second, they are often missing from the restaurant menu, but are too good not to share with people from other cultures.

Ground pork has endless uses in Chinese kitchens and is very popular with both home cooks and restaurant chefs. It is used in pork dumplings, meatballs, meat sauces and some stir-fried dishes. The Chinese prefer ground pork to ground beef simply because ground pork has a smoother texture and a richer taste, which is vitally important for making successful meatballs and tasty dumpling fillings. Another merit of using ground pork is in the time saved from mincing the pork. After spending so much energy in cutting all kinds of foods, even skillful Chinese home cooks are happy to dispense with the laborious task of mincing pork. Ground pork is also extremely economical in use. You need just a little ground pork to flavor a dish, for its rich flavor goes a long way. When stir-frying a large plate of cut vegetables, you need only a few tablespoons of marinated ground pork to give the dish a nice meaty flavor. However, when I entertain, I prefer not to stint on the pork — I usually make meatballs to give my dishes a more presentable and elegant look. In my spare time, I often make bags of pork meatballs and store them in the freezer. These frozen savory meatballs are a great time-saver when there is a party. They can be easily assembled into a formal braised dish by adding seasonal vegetables such as fresh mushrooms, snow peas or bok choy.

Ham, with its intense flavor and versatility, has found its way into many Chinese kitchens. While Smithfield ham is the top choice for many elaborate Chinese banquet dishes, I find Canadian bacon or any good brand of cooked ham extremely useful when I am out of ground pork or meat. I use ham in soups, fried rice, noodles and tossed salads for extra color and taste. This is a marvelous ingredient for Chinese cooking.

京醬肉絲

Stir-Fried Pork with Sweet Bean Paste

This dish goes well with rice, noodles, or Mu Shu pancakes. When serving with Mu Shu pancakes, be sure to add a few pieces of onion or scallion to enhance the flavor. Simple but flavorful, this dish is particularly suited for beginners and busy working people. If cutting pork into shreds is a problem for you, use ground pork.

1 1/4 pounds pork loin
1/2 small onion
1 large scallion stalk
oil for stir-frying

Marinade

2 teaspoons dry sherry
2 teaspoons soy sauce
1 tablespoon cornstarch
1 teaspoon sesame oil
2 tablespoons sweet bean
   sauce or Hoisin sauce

Seasoning Sauce

1 tablespoon sugar
2 tablespoons water or
   chicken broth
salt to taste

Method

1. Cut the pork into shreds and mix with the marinade. For a more flavorful dish, add the sweet bean sauce to the pork just before cooking. Cut the onion into thin wedges and the scallions into 1/2-inch sections.

2. Heat 4 tablespoons of oil and sauté half of the onion until light brown and fragrant. Add the pork, stirring and tossing to separate the shreds and to coat with oil.

3. When the red in the meat is completely gone, add the rest of the onion pieces and scallion sections, along with the seasoning sauce. Toss for another 2 minutes or until well blended. Remove to a serving platter and serve immediately.

6 servings

絲 瓜 炒 肉 片

Stir-Fried Pork with Chinese Okra

This is a favorite Southern dish. The taste of the pork slices improves greatly after absorbing the refreshing flavor of the vegetable. Chinese okra, the long dark green squash that has a uniquely delicate taste, can only be found in Chinese food stores (unlike American okra, this squash has a rather clean taste). If unavailable, try Kirby cucumber, which is also quite tasty with stir-fried pork.

1/2 pound lean pork
2 medium Chinese okras
oil for stir-frying
2 slices ginger
3 cloves garlic, chopped
salt and pepper to taste
1 tablespoon oyster sauce

Marinade

1 tablespoon soy sauce
1 teaspoon dry sherry
1 teaspoon sugar
1/2 tablespoon cornstarch
1 teaspoon sesame oil

Method

1. Cut the pork into thin slices and pound lightly. Then immerse in the marinade for at least 10 minutes.

2. Rinse the Chinese okras lightly. Using a paring knife or peeler, remove the rough outer skin but try to retain some green color. Cut into neat slices, showing the green part.

3. Heat 3 tablespoon of oil. Stir-fry the pork until the red is gone and the meat lightly browned. Remove and set aside.

4. Reheat the remaining oil in the wok, adding a small amount if needed. Sauté the ginger and garlic until light brown. Stir-fry the Chinese okra for a minute to coat with the flavored oil, sprinkling salt and pepper to season. Add the pork and oyster sauce, tossing to blend well. Cook for another 2 minutes or until the Chinese okra has absorbed enough flavor. Remove and serve hot.

4 servings

Note

Chinese okra is also known as angled luffa or silk squash.

什錦肉末
Rainbow Ground Pork

This colorful dish has all the taste and convenience that a family meal needs. You can please the kids even more if you add a handful of roasted peanuts or cashews.

2/3 pound ground pork
1 large green bell pepper
1 large carrot
oil for stir-frying
2 tablespoons chopped onion, divided
1 1/2 ounces frozen whole kernel corn, drained well

Marinade
1 tablespoon soy sauce
2 teaspoons dry sherry
2 teaspoons sweet bean sauce or hoisin sauce
2 teaspoons cornstarch

Seasoning Sauce
1 tablespoon oyster sauce
1 teaspoon chili bean paste
salt to taste

Cornstarch Mixture
2 tablespoons chicken broth
1 tablespoon cornstarch
1 teaspoon sesame oil

Method

1. Mix the pork with the marinade and set aside. Lightly rinse the green bell pepper and carrot. Cut into small pieces close to the size of the corn kernels.

2. Heat 3 tablespoons of oil over medium heat. Sauté half of the chopped onion until light brown. Add the pork, stirring and tossing to break lumps into bits. As the meat turns light brown, add the carrot and continue mixing to coat with sauce. Cook for about 2 minutes, then remove from the wok.

3. Clean the wok with a paper towel. Wash and dry well. Heat 3 tablespoons of oil and brown the rest of the chopped onion. Stir-fry the green bell pepper briskly for 30 seconds. Add the corn, tossing for another few seconds. Add the seasoning sauce and mix well. Return the pork and carrot to the wok and. continue mixing for about 2 minutes. Thicken with the cornstarch mixture, blend well and remove to a serving platter.

6 servings

珍珠丸子
Pearl Rice Meatballs

There are meatballs in every cuisine, but these stand out beautifully with their pearl-like rice coating and elegant taste. This is an ideal dish for entertaining. It frequently appears in Chinese New Year banquets because of its symbolic meaning — roundness signifies things coming your way.

3/4 cup sticky rice (glutinous rice)
1/2 pound ground pork
1 tablespoon minced carrots for garnish
1 tablespoon sweet peas for garnish

Marinade

1 teaspoon dry sherry
2 teaspoons soy sauce
1 teaspoon sesame oil
1/2 egg, beaten
2 teaspoons chicken broth
salt and pepper to taste
2 tablespoons cornstarch

Filling

1 teaspoon chopped scallions
1/2 teaspoon minced ginger
3 tablespoons chopped water chestnuts

Method

1. In a medium-sized bowl, cover the sticky rice with water and let it soak for an hour. Drain the rice thoroughly in a strainer. It is important that there is no trace of dripping water.

2. Mix the ground pork with the marinade and filling ingredients. Stir in a circular motion for 3~5 minutes. Stirring gives the meatballs an elastic texture.

3. Shape the pork mixture into meatballs the size of ping-pong balls and roll each meatball over the sticky rice. Place the rice-coated meatballs 1/2-inch apart on a lightly greased plate and steam over medium-high heat for 30 minutes.

4. Before serving, garnish each meatball with minced carrots and a piece of sweet pea. For a showy presentation, decorate the plate with pickled carrot slices and add tiny parsley leaves in between the carrots to complete the arrangement. Serve hot.

6 servings

Note

Sticky rice is available in Chinese stores and health food stores.

燴肉丸

Braised Pork Meatballs

Pork meatballs are not only easy to make but are also very adaptable. In whichever way you cook them, they always taste delicious. You can bake, braise, fry or cook them in soups. But don't forget to add a couple of vegetables to soak up the rich taste coming from the pork.

1/4 pound snow peas
1 cup fresh or canned straw
  mushrooms
1/4 cup sliced carrots
1 pound lean ground pork
1/3 square medium soft tofu
  for added tenderness
  (optional)
oil for stir-frying
1 tablespoon minced garlic
salt to taste
1/2 cup chicken broth

Marinade

1/2 egg, beaten
1 tablespoon soy sauce
1 tablespoon cornstarch

Seasoning Sauce

1 tablespoon soy sauce
1 teaspoon sugar
1/2 teaspoon hot bean paste
  (optional)
1 tablespoon oyster sauce

Cornstarch Mixture

1 1/2 tablespoons cornstarch
3 tablespoons water

Method

1. Remove both ends and
   strings from the snow
   peas. Rinse lightly and
   drain well. Rinse the straw
   mushrooms lightly and set
   aside. Using a cookie
   cutter, cut the carrot slices
   into floral shapes.

2. Mix the pork with the
   marinade and tofu (if
   using) for 10 minutes.
   Shape the mixture into
   balls the size of apricots.
   Heat 1 cup of oil and deep-
   fry the pork meatballs in
   two batches until golden
   brown. Drain and remove
   with a slotted spoon.
3. Pour out all but 3

tablespoons of oil. Reheat
the oil and brown the
garlic. Immediately add
the carrots, snow peas and
salt; toss for 2~3 minutes
to blend with the oil,
sprinkling with a little
chicken broth to keep the
vegetables moist. Add the
chicken broth, meatballs,
straw mushrooms and
seasoning sauce. Simmer
over medium heat for
about 3 minutes then add
the cornstarch mixture to
thicken the sauce. Remove
to a serving plate and
serve hot.

6~8 servings

冰糖排骨
Sugar-Glazed Spareribs

This is a great way to prepare meat — simple and mess-free — and also a perfect recipe for someone who loves good taste but can't afford the time for fancy cooking. You'll be amazed at the results. The flavor is just as good as barbecued meat. Rock sugar and soy sauce make a marvelous simmering sauce. You may also try it with other meats.

2 1/2 pound pork spareribs
1/3 cup rock sugar
3/4 cup soy sauce
1/4 cup water

Method

1. Have your butcher cut the spareribs into 3~4 strips. Cut the strips into chunks. Rinse lightly and place in a medium pot; add water to cover and boil for 5 minutes. Drain thoroughly but save the broth for soups. Boiling the spareribs first helps to eliminate impurities and unpleasant odors.

2. In a skillet, bring the spareribs, rock sugar, soy sauce and water to a boil. Reduce the heat to medium-low and allow it to simmer gently for 45~60 minutes. Toss occasionally to ensure even cooking. When the liquid is reduced to about 1/4 cup and the meat is tender enough, it is done. Remove to a serving plate and garnish with a few pieces of cilantro.

6 servings

Note

Rock sugar is available in gourmet stores or Chinese grocery stores. Sometimes it comes in big pieces, which makes measuring difficult. Break the sugar into smaller pieces first before measuring.

糖醋排骨
Sweet and Sour Spareribs

In the eyes of the Chinese, this dish is more tempting than the famous sweet-and-sour pork. Clearly the Chinese are partial to spareribs, which have a much deeper flavor. This is a simplified recipe for the busy modern cook. You may not get plenty of meat from spareribs, but you will be delighted with its succulence.

118

1 1/2 pounds spareribs
1 small red chili pepper
2 medium green chili peppers
oil for frying
1 tablespoon chopped garlic
1 cup pineapple chunks

Marinade

1 tablespoon soy sauce
1 tablespoon dry sherry
1 egg, beaten

Dry Coating

1/3 cup cornstarch
1/3 cup flour

Seasoning Sauce

3 tablespoons sugar
2 tablespoons vinegar
1 tablespoon soy sauce
1/3 cup chicken broth
1 tablespoon cornstarch
salt and pepper to taste

Method

1. Have your butcher cut the whole rack of spareribs into 3~4 long strips. Rinse lightly and drain well. Cut each strip between the bones into squares. Mix with the marinade for 20~30 minutes. Rinse the red and green chili peppers and cut into 1/2-inch squares.

2. Drain the spareribs and dip them in the dry coating just before frying. Heat 2 cups of oil over high heat. Deep-fry the flour-coated spareribs in small batches until golden brown. Drain and remove to a serving platter.

3. Pour out all but 2 tablespoons of oil. Heat to the smoking point and sauté the garlic for 2 seconds. Stir-fry peppers briskly for 30 seconds over high heat, then add the pineapple and mix well, about 1 minute. Remove from wok. Clean the wok and dry with a paper towel.

4. Heat 1 tablespoon of oil, add the seasoning sauce and mix lightly over low heat. Cook for about 1 minute until well blended, then turn off the heat. Return the spareribs, peppers and pineapple to the wok and coat with the sauce. Remove to a serving plate and serve hot.

6 servings

烤排骨
Barbecued Spareribs

The tantalizing taste of Chinese barbecued ribs is easier to achieve than you think. The secret lies in making the right sauce, such as the one in this recipe. As for the cooking method, there is hardly anyone in this country who doesn't know how to barbecue. This could be your house specialty once you have learned to prepare the dish

2 pounds sparerib strips
12-14 broccoli florets for garnish
1/4 cup flour

Marinade
2 tablespoons dry sherry
2 tablespoons soy sauce
1/2 tablespoon five-spice powder
1 teaspoon garlic powder
1 teaspoon minced ginger

Basting Sauce
3 tablespoons Hoisin sauce
3 tablespoons honey
2 tablespoons catsup
1 teaspoon garlic powder
1 tablespoon oil

Method
1. Rinse and drain the spareribs. Mix the spareribs with the marinade and let stand at least 4~5 hours or overnight. Meanwhile, blanch the broccoli florets in a pot of boiling water for about two minutes. Immediately transfer to a bowl containing ice cold water— this helps to preserve the bright green color in broccoli.

2. Coat the spareribs evenly with the basting sauce (keep the balance for basting) and then sprinkle lightly with flour. If you can find a reliable Chinese barbecue sauce from a Chinese market, you may also use it as a substitute for this sauce.

3. Bake the spareribs at 450°F for 20 minutes then turn the heat down to 350°F. When the spareribs turn brown, brush on the rest of the basting sauce plus 1 tablespoon of oil as the final coating.

4. Continue to bake until very brown, about 20~30 minutes. Transfer to a serving plate and garnish with the blanched broccoli florets. Serve hot or cold.

6 servings

香煎豬排
Scrumptious Sautéed Pork Chops

Fried pork chops are rarely served in my house because of health reasons. However, when planning a party menu for a group of youngsters, taste usually outweighs nutrition. The aroma of fried pork chops is irresistible and it is always the first dish to disappear. To balance the nutrition and to ease your feelings of guilt, try to serve a variety of vegetarian dishes along with the pork chops.

4-6 pieces pork chops
salt and pepper to taste
1/2 cup sweet potato flour or
    cornstarch
oil for deep-frying
leafy greens for garnish

Marinade

2 teaspoons soy sauce
1 tablespoon dry sherry
1 1/4 tablespoon sugar
1 tablespoon chopped
    scallions
1 tablespoon chopped ginger
4 cloves garlic, crushed

Method

1. Lightly rinse the pork and drain well. To tenderize the meat, use the blade of a heavy knife or cleaver to pound both sides of the pork chops. Lightly sprinkle salt and pepper all over the meat. Then place the chops in a mixing bowl, add the marinade and set aside to marinate for at least two hours.

2. Before frying, drain the pork chops well. Then coat each piece with sweet potato flour and line it on the cutting board.

3. In a medium-sized frying pan, heat 2/3 cup of oil over medium-high heat. Shallow-fry 2~3 pork chops at a time. Brown both sides nicely until thoroughly cooked and aromatic. Repeat with the rest of the pork chops. When done, remove to a serving plate lined with leafy greens and serve immediately.

4~6 servings

Note

Sweet potato flour, which yields crispier crust, can be purchased from Chinese markets.

BEEF : THE EMERGING TASTE

Beef was rarely seen on dinner tables when I was growing up in Taiwan during the fifties. Things have changed significantly since then. Nowadays beef is just as common as other meats in Chinese households. More and more Chinese youngsters are influenced by Western diet, putting pressure on moms to conform by cooking hamburgers and steaks. But for the older Chinese, traditions still prevail. In the hands of an experienced cook, there can indeed be a multitude of ways to prepare a delicious beef dish. In addition to beef stir-fries, the chinese have elaborate beef stews, beef cold cuts, aromatic beef dumplings, beef egg rolls, crisp or tender meat balls, and much more.

Stir-frying seems to be designed specially for beef, which cooks rather quickly. This method is a real saver in time, money and calories. A chunk of sirloin steak serves only one; if cut into thin strips and stir-fried with a head of broccoli, it will serve at least 3 to 4 persons.

The hearty flavor of beef goes well with almost any vegetable. The most popular accompanying vegetables for beef are usually the ones with strong flavors, such as green bell peppers, scallions and celery. Greens with a refreshing taste, such as asparagus, green beans and snow peas, are also good combinations.

Unlike pork, beef demands more care in stir-frying or you could end up with tough and tasteless meat. Many inexperienced cooks fail to produce the required tenderness and smoothness because they lack the skill to prepare beef the proper way.

To keep stir-fried beef tender and juicy, follow these guidelines:

* Flank steak is the best choice if it is fresh, but if unavailable or not so fresh use other tender cuts such as sirloin or tenderloin.

* Cut against the grain for better texture.

* Allow the beef to absorb enough liquid (soy sauce, sherry and a small amount of oil) during marinating (30 minutes or longer). Marinating gives the beef a tender and juicy taste. Mixing continuously will bring the desired result. Adding a small amount of baking soda to the marinade is a method used by restaurants to tenderize beef. Adding a littel sugar and vinegar also works; but be sure to rinse out the vinegar before adding marinade to the beef.

Apart from using these special techniques, another important factor is the sauce. A dish is usually named after its sauce. Other than soy sauce, the most popular seasoning sauces for stir-fried beef are oyster sauce, fermented black bean sauce and sha cha sauce. If you like a stronger taste, use chili bean sauce. This is one of the most robust seasonings that can add zest to just about any dish.

Ground beef may receive less attention than whole beef in the average Chinese household; nevertheless, it stars in a few famous dim sum dishes such as Cantonese steamed beef meatballs and Northern-style crispy beef pancakes. In many cases, beef may be used the same way as ground pork if measures are taken to eliminate its strong taste and improve its texture.

Here are some "secret" methods that the Chinese use to improve the taste and texture of beef:

* Use Sichuan peppercorn oil, minced ginger and scallions to combat the gamy taste.

* Mix in egg, cornstarch and sesame oil for added smoothness. Interestingly, Crispy Beef Pancake (recipe on page 28), a famous dish made with ground beef, is often favored over egg rolls. These dumplings are juicy and flavorful on the inside, aromatic and crusty on the outside.

One advantage of Chinese cooking is its ability to transform uninteresting tough cuts of meats into delicacies. A good example of this is the popular beef stew noodles, which are made with beef shin or brisket. This Sichuan dish is well liked nationwide. When it is cooked to perfection, it tastes robust and incredibly delicious. Another famous beef shin dish is five-spice beef. It is succulent and aromatic, and the beef is usually cut into large slices and served as a first course in a banquet or as cold cuts. Offal like beef tongue and beef tripe can also be prepared in the same fashion.

Here is the key to a successful beef shin dish:

* Boil the beef in hot water (with wine and ginger) until almost tender.

* Transfer the beef to another pot with soy sauce-based liquid and cook with these spices: star anise, cinnamon sticks, dried orange peel, sugar, ginger, onion and chili bean paste until flavorful.

青椒牛肉絲
Stir-Fried Beef with Green Chili Peppers

Green bell pepper beef is a favorite dish in both Chinese restaurants and home kitchens. Green chili pepper beef is even more tempting. Whether you like hot food or not, this dish is too good to miss. Try using only half the chili peppers if you are really intimidated by their fiery taste. Even a touch of those fragrant hot peppers can make a noticeable difference in your beef.

1 pound flank steak or
   tender cut of beef
4 medium green chili peppers
oil for stir-frying
3 cloves garlic, crushed

Marinade
2 teaspoons dry sherry
1 teaspoon sesame oil
1 tablespoon soy sauce
2 teaspoons sugar
2 teaspoons oyster sauce, or
1/2 teaspoon sha cha sauce
   (optional)
1 tablespoon cornstarch
1 teaspoon shredded fresh
   ginger

Method
1. Bring the beef to a half-frozen state. Cut in half lengthwise, then cut each strip into thin slices. Stack 3~4 slices and cut into shreds. Mix with the marinade continuously for 2~3 minutes. This will keep the beef moist and tender during cooking. Let stand for 20~30 minutes.

2. Rinse the green chili peppers lightly. Be extremely careful when cutting hot peppers—the peppery juice can "burn" your hand, causing discomfort for hours. It is best to keep your hands away from the hot peppers once they are cut open. A fork may be used to handle the peppers directly. Cut into long strips. Discard the seeds if you want to minimize the hot taste.

3. Heat 5 tablespoons of oil until very hot. Sauté the garlic and green chili peppers for a few seconds. Immediately add the beef, stirring constantly to mix with the peppers and hot oil. Sprinkle a little soy sauce if needed. Cook until the red in the beef is completely gone. Remove and serve hot.

Yield:
4~6 servings

滑蛋牛肉
Quick-Fried Beef with Egg

This dish is different from Egg Fu Rong (Foo Young). Although the beef is fried twice, it still retains its tenderness. The egg not only functions as a protective coating for the beef but also adds a contrasting color and smooth texture to the dish. With the addition of a little tomato, this dish becomes even more delicious and attractive.

1/2 pound flank steak or tenderloin steak tail
1 small tomato
oil for stir-frying
salt to taste
1 stalk chopped scallions, white and green parts separated
5 large eggs, well beaten

Marinade
1 tablespoon soy sauce
1 teaspoon dry sherry
1 teaspoon sesame oil
1/2 egg white, beaten
1 tablespoon cornstarch
salt and pepper to taste

Method
1. Cut the beef into slices about 1-inch long and 1/3-inch thick . Mix the beef with the marinade continuously for about 3 minutes or until the liquid is well absorbed. Let stand for at least 15 minutes.

2. Cut the tomato into thin wedges. In a wok, heat 1 tablespoon of oil over medium high heat. Stir-fry the tomato with a pinch of salt until tender. Remove and clean the wok well.

3. Heat 3~4 tablespoons of oil over high heat then sauté half the white part of the scallions until aromatic. Add the beef immediately, stirring briskly to coat with hot oil. When the red is almost gone, remove with a slotted spoon. Pour out the remaining oil.

Clean the wok with a paper towel, then wash with water and dry well.

4. Combine the beef, the cooked tomato, salt and the green part of the scallions with the egg. Heat 4~5 tablespoons of oil to the smoking point then sizzle the remaining white part of the scallions until aromatic. Quickly add the beef and egg mixture, stirring gently to allow the mixture to form a creamy, runny sauce; do not let it get too firm. Remove and serve immediately.

4 servings

四季豆炒牛肉

Stir-Fried Beef with Green Beans

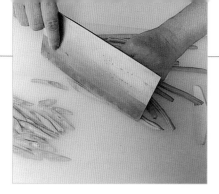

This is a typical home-style dish. After exchanging flavors, the beef and the green beans taste marvelous. The purpose of French-cutting the green beans is to expose them to more heat and flavor, thus shortening cooking time and keeping the color green. For variety, try combining the French-cut green beans with other meats.

1/2 pound flank steak or
    tender cuts of beef
1 pound fresh tender green
    beans
oil for stir-frying
2 teaspoons chopped garlic

Marinade
1 tablespoon soy sauce
1 teaspoon dry sherry
1 teaspoon sesame oil
2 teaspoons cornstarch
salt and pepper to taste

Method
1. Cut the beef into strips, mix with the marinade and set aside for 20~30 minutes. Rinse the green beans lightly. Remove the ends and strings, then diagonally cut (French-cut) each bean into 3~4 pieces.

2. Heat 4 tablespoons of oil and stir-fry the green beans until slightly limp, about 3 minutes. Drain and remove with a slotted spoon.

3. Reheat the oil over high heat. Sauté the garlic until fragrant. Add the beef and stir-fry briskly until the red is completely gone. Add the green beans and mix with the beef to coat with flavor. Cook for another 1~2 minutes. When the green beans are glazed with the rich taste of meat sauce, they are done. Remove to a serving platter and serve hot.

4~6 servings

菫菜炒牛肉
Stir-Fried Beef with Celery

Beef blends marvelously with fragrant vegetables such as celery, onion and green bell peppers. After sautéing, the raw taste of celery disappears. It becomes crunchy and aromatic, complementing the beef in taste and texture wonderfully.

2/3 pound flank steak or
    tender cuts of beef
3~4 large stalks celery
oil for stir-frying
1 tablespoon chopped garlic,
    divided
salt and pepper to taste
1/2 tablespoons sugar

Marinade
2 teaspoons dry sherry
2 tablespoons soy sauce
1 teaspoon sesame oil
1 tablespoon cornstarch

Method
1. Cut the beef into slices or shreds and place in the marinade for 15~20 minutes, mixing continuously for the first 2 minutes to allow the beef to absorb the moisture. Peel the tough strings off the celery; rinse lightly and cut into diagonal pieces.

2. Heat 2 tablespoons of oil over high heat. Sizzle half the garlic until light brown. Add the celery and stir briskly for about 2 minutes; sprinkle salt, pepper and sugar to taste. Remove when the celery is well coated with flavor. Clean the wok with water or paper towels. Dry well.

3. Heat 4 tablespoons of oil over a medium-high heat. Sauté the remaining garlic until light brown. Add the beef and stir-fry over high heat until the red is gone. Return the celery to the wok and toss to mix with the beef and sauce, about 1~2 minutes. Remove to a serving platter and serve hot.

4 servings

蔥爆牛肉

Stir-Fried Beef with Scallions

Many stir-fried meat dishes with vegetables require cooking the vegetables and meat separately, but this one is an exception. Because the scallions cook in seconds, you can cook two ingredients in one step. The trick to making this dish tender and fragrant is to buy a tender cut of beef, tenderize it and use plenty of scallions.

3/4 pound flank steak or very tender cut of beef
1 teaspoon baking soda
2 large stalks scallions
oil for stir-frying
4 cloves garlic, crushed

Marinade

1 1/2 tablespoons soy sauce
2 teaspoons dry sherry
1 1/2 teaspoons corn oil
1/2 egg white, beaten
1 1/2 tablespoons cornstarch

Method

1. Bring the beef to a half-frozen stage. First, cut into thin slices; then cut the slices (4~5 in a stack) into strips. Mix the baking soda with the beef and allow it to sit for about 10 minutes. Add 1/2 cup of water and rinse out the soda, draining well. Then place the beef in the marinade and mix continuously with a fork for 2 minutes. This will keep the beef moist and tender during cooking. Let stand for about 10 minutes. Meanwhile, rinse the scallions well then cut into 1-inch lengths.

2. Heat 4 tablespoons of oil over high heat. Sauté the garlic and a few pieces of scallion stems until the color changes. Add the beef, stirring and tossing to coat with the oil. When the red begins to disappear, add the scallions and mix the flavors together. Stir continuously to heat through. The perfect time to end the cooking is when the beef is done but the scallions are still green and firm. Remove to a serving platter and serve immediately.

2~4 servings

粉蒸牛肉

Steamed Rice-Coated Beef

All rice-coated meat dishes are extremely tasty and well liked by the Chinese. Since steamed pork with rice coating is so popular, I have decided to include a similar version in this chapter. Here the beef is first stewed until tender, then covered with a spiced rice coating and steamed for another hour. The end result is a melt-in-your-mouth, tender and aromatic beef.

2 pounds shin beef with bone
4 cups water
2~3 slices ginger
1 small onion, cut into
   wedges
1 tablespoon oil for sautéing
2 yam or red skin potatoes
4 small packages spiced rice
   powder
2 teaspoons sesame oil

Seasonings

1/3 cup rice wine
2 tablespoons soy sauce
1 tablespoon sugar
3 stars anise
2 sticks cinnamon sticks
1 can chicken broth

Method

1. Rinse the beef well and cut
   into bite-sized pieces.
   Place the beef in a stewing
   pot, add the seasonings
   and water and bring to a
   boil. Maintain a gentle
   boil, stirring occasionally.
   Meanwhile, in a small pan,
   brown the ginger and
   onion briefly with 1
   tablespoon of oil for extra
   flavor. Add this to the beef
   stew and cook until very
   tender, about 1 1/2 hour.
   Remove and drain the
   cooked beef; save the sauce
   for the next step.

2. Here the yam is used to
   catch the flavorful juices
   dripped from the beef.
   First, peel the yam and cut
   into bite-sized pieces. Line
   the bottom of a large
   heatproof glassware or
   soup bowl with the yam
   pieces. Cut the rice powder
   bags open and pour the
   rice powder into a dish.
   Roll each piece of the
   cooked beef over the rice
   powder and place on top of
   the yam. Repeat until all
   the beef pieces are coated
   and stacked loosely like a
   dome. Pour about 1 cup of
   the stewing sauce over the
   rice-coated beef and drizzle
   the sesame oil on top.
   Place the bowl in a
   steamer and steam for an
   hour or until the beef
   becomes very tender. Serve
   hot.

8 servings

Note:

**Five-spice rice powder
comes in a small paper
box, which can be
purchased from a
Chinese food market.**

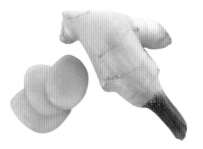

蘿蔔紅燒牛肉

Red-Cooked Beef with Daikon

This is a simple version of the famous beef stew that many Chinese adore. My picky husband is one who could never get tired of it. He holds the record of cooking this same dish for a whopping 5 months while I was away on a trip to Taiwan. Although the taste of this dish is irresistibly tempting, the cooking procedure is fairly simple. Besides serving with rice, it tastes great with noodles or pastas.

2 pounds beef shin (with or without bones)
1 slice ginger
1/4 cup rice wine
1 large daikon
1 large carrot

Seasonings

1 cup water
1/2 cup rice wine or dry sherry
3~4 thick slices ginger
2 tablespoons soy sauce
1/3 cup tomato juice for added color
1/2 small onion, cut into wedges
2 stars anise
1 stick cinnamon stick
2~4 dried chili peppers (optional)

Method

1. Rinse the beef lightly then place in a deep pot. Add a slice of ginger, 1/4 cup of rice wine and water to cover. Boil over high heat for 5 minutes and remove to cool slightly. Using a colander, drain the beef and reserve the broth. The purpose of this step is to eliminate some fat and impurities and to make cutting easier. Cut the boiled beef into large chunks.

2. Place the beef chunks in another pot. Add the beef broth and seasonings; cook over medium-low heat for about an hour or until almost tender. Meanwhile, peel both the daikon and carrot and cut into chunks. Add these chunks to the simmering beef and cook for another 30~40 minutes, mixing occasionally for even cooking. When the meat and vegetables are both tender and flavorful, remove to a serving platter and serve immediately.

6 servings

沙茶牛肉串
Skewered Beef with Sha Cha Sauce

Internationally popular, this aromatic dish has a few Chinese versions and this is one of the best liked. Sha cha sauce, which is effective in masking the gamy taste in meat, seems to blend exceptionally well with beef and lamb, although you can also use it with seafood and pork. For the adventurous cook, try this recipe with other meats.

1 1/2 pounds stewing beef
2 medium green bell peppers
2 small orange bell peppers
2 medium onions
1 bag of 12-inch bamboo
   skewers

Marinade
2 tablespoons Sha Cha sauce
2 tablespoons soy sauce
2 tablespoons dry sherry
1 teaspoon garlic powder
1 tablespoon sugar
salt and pepper to taste
2 teaspoons sesame oil
1 medium onion, cut into
   wedges
6 slices ginger

Method
1. Rinse the beef lightly and drain well. Immerse the beef in the marinade and let it soak for at least two hours or overnight. Drain the beef and save the marinade for the vegetables. Soak the bamboo skewers in water for at least 30 minutes to prevent burning.

2. Rinse the bell peppers and onions lightly. Cut the green bell peppers and onion into cubes to match the size of the beef. Cut one orange bell pepper into cubes and the other into rings for garnish. Place the onion and bell pepper cubes (not the bell pepper rings) in a bowl and pour the beef marinade on top. Allow them to marinate for 20~30 minutes or longer, with occasional turning.

3. Now spear the beef and vegetables on the skewers, about 3~4 pieces of meat and 6~10 pieces each of onion and pepper on each stick —spear the meat and vegetables alternately, or in any way you prefer.

4. To cook the beef, you have the options of baking, broiling or sautéing. Although baking is the most convenient method, broiling and sautéing will yield better results. Whichever way you choose, cook until the meat turns light brown. Serve hot.

4~6 servings

中式烤牛肉
Roast Beef Chinese Style

There is hardly any roast beef in Chinese cuisine. By luck I found this recipe, which combines Western techniques with Chinese spices and sauces. The end result is an extra-rich tasting roast beef with a character of its own. I enjoyed it as a reward for my adventurous experimentation.

2 1/2 pounds bottom round
    beef

Marinade
2 teaspoons five-spice powder
1/2 tablespoon salt
1 teaspoon pepper

Basting Sauce
2 tablespoons hoisin sauce
2 tablespoons honey
1 tablespoon catsup
1 teaspoon soy sauce

1/2 tablespoons garlic powder
1/2 cup flour

Method
1. Sprinkle the marinade evenly over the beef and allow it to marinate overnight or longer. Before roasting, brush the beef with the basting sauce and sprinkle evenly with flour.

2. Bake at 450°F for the first 20 minutes then reduce to 325°F and bake until brown. Remove and cool to room temperature. Cut into slices. Serve as a main dish with rice, noodles or bread.

6~8 servings

CHICKEN AND DUCK :
LEGACY OF THE ANCIENT CHINESE

Chicken rightfully deserves its universal popularity. It is the most tasty and healthful meat in our diet. Chicken also ranks high in its versatility and adaptability. This quality is well reflected in a little Chinese anecdote that has amused many people. There was once a poor and hungry beggar who, out of necessity, had stolen a chicken. Having no cooking utensils and afraid of being caught, this fellow cleverly wrapped the chicken with mud and buried it in hot sand. To his amazement, the chicken turned out to be a most juicy and flavorful dish. And this was how the famous recipe "Beggar's Chicken" originated. The story proves one point — any cook with just a little imagination can easily turn chicken, with its superior taste, into a great dish.

Though boneless chicken dishes are quite popular among Westerners — for example, "General's Chicken" and "Stir-fried Chicken with Mushrooms"

(Moo Gu Gai Pien) — native Chinese tend to be partial to chicken with bones, which they feel have a deeper flavor than boneless chicken. Red-cooked chicken, soy sauce chicken, steamed chicken and chicken soup are among the best loved chicken dishes. Years ago, a pot of well-made chicken soup was deemed the ultimate delight and a nourishing food for women after childbirth. In those days, making ginseng chicken soup was also a common way for a woman to show her love for her husband or children.

Recently, stir-fried chicken breast (or thigh) is becoming more popular in Chinese households because of the profusion of packaged chicken parts at supermarkets. Chicken breast is excellent for stir-frying because it cooks in just minutes. However, you need to use special care when handling this delicate part. Once overcooked, chicken breast becomes dry and bland. To prevent

overcooking, marinade chicken breast with a small amount of oil, egg white and cornstarch (some chefs use sugar or baking soda). This coating helps to seal in the juices and protects the meat from the high searing heat. But do remember to remove the chicken breast from the heat once it is no longer pink.

When a dish calls for diced chicken or chicken chunks, it is best to use chicken thighs or legs. These parts might demand a little more effort in cutting than the breast (the best time to cut chicken is when it is half frozen), but the resulting satisfying taste is well worth it. Although the deep, rich taste of "General's Chicken" is due largely to skillful stir-frying and proper blending of seasonings, the appeal of this dish would be lost without the tender, elastic texture of chicken legs (or thighs).

Long before Buffalo Wings appeared on the scene, the

Chinese had already made chicken wings a delicacy by cooking them with elaborate sauces and herbs. Well-cooked wings are a real treat for people who look for flavor. In fact, the Chinese cook wings very much the same way as Westerners cook other parts of the chicken. The basic technique is browning, after which the chicken is simmered with various seasonings, herbs and spices until tender and flavorful.

Chinese home cooks in this country are also very adaptable. Some of them adopt Western cooking methods in order to save time while others do it because they try to create diversity in flavor. Thus, barbecuing has become a very popular form of cooking in some Chinese homes. Usually the chicken wings are marinated overnight with a rich combination of seasonings, such as ginger, garlic, scallions, sherry, soy sauce, sugar and five-spice powder. Grilled wings are tender, juicy and exceedingly delicious. They are excellent finger foods for parties.

Compared to chicken, duck is less popular in Chinese home kitchens even though the Chinese are known for cooking the best duck dishes. It could be the sheer size and the high fat content of this fowl that have turned many eager cooks away. Nonetheless, duck has a special quality that few people have noticed — its skin can be easily roasted or deep-fried to a golden crispy crust. It is this wonderful property of the skin that has elevated the duck to the star status of the Peking Duck. Duck meat also has a deep, subtle taste when it is skillfully prepared. Interestingly, duck is seldom stir-fried, but it is used in rosasted, stewed, soup and braised dishes.

Very few Chinese would attempt to make Peking Duck at home, partly because of the elaborate preparation involved and partly because a huge special oven is needed to roast the skin to perfection. Instead, they prefer a smaller version of "Crispy-Skin Duck," which is relatively simple, but just as fabulous.

Here is the good news for those who love to cook duck, but are unwilling to handle the whole bird. For the last few years, I have had the good fortune of buying packaged duck legs at some large Chinese food markets. This has made my cooking job so much easier and has given me a large portion of meat. I wish my readers luck in finding this great product.

豆豉炒雞丁

Diced Chicken with Fermented Black Beans

Fermented black beans are a powerful seasoning — only a very small amount is required to add depth to a dish. The key to making tender diced chicken in this recipe is to use the thigh or leg. These parts retain their tenderness longer than other parts and are easier to work with.

1 pound chicken thighs
2~3 Kirby cucumbers or
    Chinese cucumbers
1 tablespoon black beans
oil for stir-frying
2 tablespoons chopped garlic
salt and pepper to taste
4~5 slices red chili pepper for
    garnish

Marinade

2 teaspoons dry sherry
salt and pepper to taste
1 tablespoon light soy sauce
1 tablespoon cornstarch

Seasoning Sauce

1 teaspoon dry sherry
1 teaspoon soy sauce
l teaspoon sugar
1 teaspoon chili bean sauce
    (optional)
1/3 cup water or chicken
    broth

Method

1. Trim fat off the chicken thighs and cut into cubes. Mix with the marinade and let stand for 10~20 minutes. Rinse the cucumbers well; cut away any blemishes, then cut into small pieces the size of bouillon cubes. Soak the black beans for 1 minute; drain well and cut into finer pieces.

2. Heat 2 tablespoons of oil and sauté the garlic until light brown. Add the cucumbers, sprinkle with salt and pepper and continue stirring for about 2 minutes, then remove.

3. Clean and dry the wok well. Heat 3 tablespoons of oil until very hot. Immediately add the chicken, tossing to mix and brown lightly. Cover and continue to brown in oil for 3 minutes. Now return the cooked cucumbers to the wok, mixing quickly with the chicken while adding the seasoning sauce. Allow to simmer over medium heat for another 2 minutes or until the liquid is reduced to about half and the food is well coated with flavor. Remove and serve hot.

4 servings

蒜味雞翅

Sautéed Garlic Chicken Wings

It is amazing how a few pieces of garlic browned in oil can add so much aroma to chicken wings. Although garlic is the main seasoning, the final dish does not have a garlicky taste at all.

10~12 chicken wings
oil for stir-frying
10 cloves garlic, crushed
5 slices ginger
1 small onion, sliced

Seasoning Sauce
2 tablespoons dry sherry
2 tablespoons soy sauce
1 tablespoon sugar
1/3 cup water or chicken
    broth

Method

1. Cut chicken wings in halves. Rinse and drain; dry with cloth or paper towels.

2. Heat 3 tablespoons of oil over high heat. Sauté the garlic, ginger and onion briefly, about 5 seconds. Immediately add the chicken wings and toss to mix with hot oil. Allow the chicken to brown in oil, with the lid on, over high heat. Stir occasionally to prevent scorching.

3. When the chicken wings are fragrant and brown, add the seasoning sauce. Cover and simmer over medium heat for about 10 minutes, tossing occasionally to mix with sauce. Remove to a serving platter. Serve warm or cold.

4~6 servings

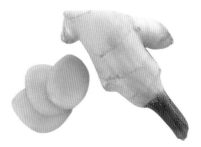

酸辣雞球

Hot and Sour Chicken

This is a home version of a Sichuan dish, hot and spicy, but on the milder side. I like recipes that can go both ways and ones which you can adjust to taste. If you like the taste a little more robust, by all means increase the amount of spices. You may also use chicken breast, if desired.

6 chicken drumsticks
oil for frying
1/2 small onion, cut into
    wedges
1/2 tablespoon minced garlic
2 stalks scallions, cut into 1-
    inch sections

Marinade

2 tablespoon rice wine or dry
    sherry
1 tablespoon light soy sauce
1/3 teaspoon pepper
1 tablespoon minced garlic
1 tablespoon cornstarch
    mixed with 1/4 cup water

Seasoning Sauce

1 cup chicken broth
1 teaspoon lemon juice
2 teaspoons vinegar
1 tablespoon sugar
1/2 teaspoon chili paste or
    Tabasco
salt and pepper to taste

Cornstarch Mixture

2 teaspoons cornstarch
2 tablespoons water

Method

1. Bring the drumsticks to a
   half-frozen state for easier
   cutting. Cut and discard
   the bottom joint of the
   drumsticks; cut each piece
   into 2~3 neat portions.
   Immerse the drumsticks in
   the marinade and let sit
   for at least 30 minutes or
   longer. Drain thoroughly
   before cooking and save
   the marinade for the final
   sauce.

2. In a wok, heat 1/3 cup of
   oil over high heat. Brown
   the onion briefly, then add
   the well-drained chicken,
   tossing quickly to coat
   with oil and heat. Lower
   the heat slightly and

continue mixing and
turning the chicken in oil
until lightly browned.
Remove with a slotted
spoon and drain the oil
well. Pick out and discard
the wilted onion.

3. Pour out all but 1
   tablespoon of oil. Reheat
   the wok and lightly brown
   the minced garlic. Add half
   of the leftover marinade
   and all the seasoning
   sauce ingredients and
   simmer for 1 minute. Add
   the chicken and scallions,
   tossing to mix the flavors
   together. Thicken the
   sauce with the cornstarch
   mixture and remove to a
   serving platter. Serve
   immediately.

4~6 servings

鼓油雞
Soy Sauce Chicken

This tender and aromatic Cantonese dish has many fans from other regions, including myself. I have tried several versions but finally settled on this one from my sister-in-law. I like the simplicity and the glistening color. The secret of the tenderness comes from a very special cooking technique — boiling the chicken briefly, then steeping for a couple of hours in a robust sauce. And instead of relying completely on soy sauce, the recipe has borrowed some reddish color from catsup and tomato. A marvelous innovation!

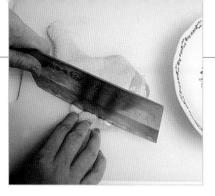

6 chicken legs
1 ripe tomato, cut into wedges

Marinade
1/4 cup dry sherry
2 slices ginger

Seasoning Sauce
1 cup Chinese cooking wine
3/4 cup soy sauce (Chinese brands preferred)
2 cups water
1/3 cup rock sugar or regular sugar
3 large slices ginger
1 tablespoon catsup, for improved color
2 stars anise, or 1 tablespoon Sichuan peppercorns
2 cinnamon sticks

Method

1. Trim the fat off the chicken, rinse lightly and drain well. Marinate with dry sherry and ginger for 15~30 minutes, turning occasionally to coat with flavor.

2. In a medium-sized stockpot boil the seasoning sauce and tomato wedges over medium heat for 5 minutes or until the liquid becomes flavorful. Add the chicken, with the marinade, to the sauce and cook for 6~8 minutes with the pot half-covered. Turn off the heat, cover the pot and allow the chicken to steep in the sauce for 20~30 minutes. Then turn the heat on again and cook for another 3 minutes. Allow the chicken to sit in the hot sauce with the heat turned off for at least an hour or longer.

3. After cooking slowly in the hot sauce, the chicken becomes tender and flavorful. Let cool slightly, then remove the chicken from the sauce and cut into 1/2-inch pieces. Serve as a main course or as a cold cut.

8~10 servings

椒鹽雞
Sichuan Peppercorn Chicken

This remarkable family recipe, though simple in preparation, deserves to be served in a banquet. The nice part of it is its versatility. After marinating, you can steam, bake, sauté or deep-fry it. Any way you cook it, it tastes wonderful. Using chicken legs makes cooking and cutting much easier. If desired, you may use a whole chicken. This is almost a foolproof recipe; the trick is to marinate for about 2 to 3 days before cooking.

3 tablespoons Sichuan
  peppercorns
4 chicken legs
1 1/2 tablespoon salt
1 tablespoon flour for light
  coating
oil for sautéing

Method

1. Heat the wok over medium heat without adding any oil. Stir-fry the peppercorns briskly for 20~30 seconds or until brown and smoky. Let cool for a few minutes.

2. Trim the fat off the chicken legs. It is not necessary to rinse the chicken legs, but make sure they are dried properly. Sprinkle salt generously all over the chicken and then rub the peppercorns all over, pressing down so that all parts of the chicken are evenly coated with salt and peppercorns. Refrigerate the marinated chicken for at least 2~3 days to allow the flavor to penetrate.

3. Before cooking, wash the peppercorns and salt off the chicken and drain thoroughly. Place the chicken legs in a steamer and steam for about 30 minutes or until done. Let cool for 10 minutes. Drain thoroughly and dust lightly with flour.

4. Heat 4 tablespoons of oil and sauté the chicken until lightly crisp and golden brown. Remove to cool. Cut each leg into 4~5 pieces. Serve warm or cold.

6 servings

蘆筍拌雞絲
Chicken and Asparagus Salad

There are not many chicken salad dishes in Chinese cuisine, but what few we have are always elegant. This is a great tasting chicken salad. The lightly poached chicken strips are so tender and tasty and they match beautifully with the tender-crisp asparagus. Insist on using the best asparagus. If it is not in season, substitute celery.

1/2 pound boneless, skinless chicken breast
2/3 teaspoon vinegar
1 teaspoon sugar
2~3 thin slices ginger (optional)
1/2 pound tender fresh asparagus
1 1/2 cups chicken broth
oil for sautéing

Marinade
1 teaspoon dry sherry
1/2 teaspoon soy sauce
1/4 teaspoon sesame oil
2 teaspoons cornstarch

Chicken Sauce
2 teaspoons Sichuan peppercorns
1/2 cup chicken broth
2 stalks cilantro, well rinsed
2/3 teaspoon sugar
1/4 teaspoon chili sauce (optional)
salt and pepper to taste

Cornstarch Mixture
2/3 teaspoon cornstarch
1 1/2 tablespoons water

Method

1. Cut the chicken breast into thin strips. Add the vinegar and sugar, mix thoroughly and let sit for about 10 minutes. Rinse lightly and drain thoroughly. This will make the chicken strips very tender. Add the marinade and ginger slices and set aside. Meanwhile, break off any tough ends of the asparagus and rinse well.

2. In a saucepan, boil the asparagus in the chicken broth for about 2 minutes until heated through. Remove the asparagus, drain well and transfer to a serving platter. Bring the chicken broth to a rolling boil. Add the chicken strips, stirring gently to separate the meat. As soon as the color changes, turn off the heat and let sit for 2 minutes. Pick out and discard the ginger slices. Remove the chicken strips with a slotted spoon and drain thoroughly. Spread the chicken strips on top of the asparagus.

3. To make the chicken sauce: In a wok, heat 1 tablespoon of oil over medium heat. Sauté the Sichuan peppercorns until light brown, remove and discard. Add the chicken broth, cilantro, sugar, chili sauce (if using), salt and pepper to the flavored oil and cook over low heat for 2 minutes to blend the flavors together. Thicken with the cornstarch mixture. Pour the sauce over the chicken strips. Serve warm or cold.

4 servings

雞絲燴白菜
Braised Chicken with Cabbage

Here is a light and tasty dish for family meals as well as for entertaining. In addition to rice, it tastes excellent with Mu Shu pork pancakes. It can also make a good filling for egg rolls and steamed buns.

2/3 pound boneless, skinless chicken breast
2 pieces large dried Chinese mushrooms
2 pounds napa cabbage
oil for stir-frying
1 teaspoon chopped garlic
1 small carrot, shredded
2/3 cup chicken broth

Marinade

2 teaspoons dry sherry
1 tablespoon light soy sauce
1 tablespoon cornstarch

Seasoning Sauce

1 tablespoon soy sauce
2 tablespoons oyster sauce
1 teaspoon sesame oil
salt and pepper to taste

Cornstarch Mixture

2 tablespoons cornstarch
3 tablespoons water

Method

1. Cut the chicken breast along the grain into thin strips and place in the marinade for at least 20 minutes. Soak the mushrooms in 1 cup of water for 15 minutes or until fully expanded. Drain well and cut into thin strips. Rinse the cabbage and drain thoroughly. Cut the stems into strips and save the leaves for soups.

2. Heat 6 tablespoons of oil over medium-high heat. Stir-fry the chicken until the color just begins to change. Drain and remove with a slotted spoon. Set aside.

3. Reheat the oil over high heat. Sauté the garlic and stir-fry the mushrooms for 1 minute. Add the cabbage stems and carrot shreds and toss for 1~2 minutes to blend well. Add the seasoning sauce and stir-fry for another 2 minutes.

4. Add the chicken broth. Simmer for 3~5 minutes or until the cabbage is tender. Add the chicken and cornstarch mixture. Bring to a boil and remove immediately. Serve hot.

6 servings

Steamed Cornish Hen with Dried Chinese Mushrooms

Steamed Cornish Hen with Dried Chinese Mushrooms, this may be the easiest chicken recipe in Chinese cuisine. Almost anyone can cook it with success. Steaming yields a light yet subtle taste that pleases many gourmets. Both the broth and chicken are delectable. The tender texture of cornish hen makes it an ideal choice for this recipe.

1-1 1/4 pounds Cornish hen
6~8 medium dried Chinese
    mushrooms

Marinade

3 tablespoons dry sherry
2 teaspoons soy sauce
3~4 slices ginger
salt and pepper to taste

Garnish

1/2 teaspoons sesame oil
1 tablespoon chopped
scallions or cilantro

Method

1. Clean and trim fat off the chicken. Cut into bite-sized pieces and marinate with the sherry, soy sauce, ginger salt and pepper for 5~10 minutes. Soak the mushrooms in 1 cup of cold water until they have fully expanded. Cut off and discard the stems because they are too tough to eat. Save both the mushrooms and the soaking liquid for the dish.

2. Place the chicken pieces in a soup bowl. Spread the ginger slices and mushrooms (with the soaking liquid) neatly on top and steam over high heat for 25~30 minutes or until the pink disappears completely. Before serving, add the sesame oil and scallions for added aroma. Serve hot.

3~4 servings

Note

To intensify the taste of this dish, simply add a can of chicken broth to the soup. You will be pleased with the result.

香酥鴨

Crisp-Skin Duck

Many Chinese feel that this dish tastes just as good as Peking Duck but requires much less effort to prepare. You don't need a lot of skill to make this great dish and it is worthwhile for the adventurous beginner to give it a try. The important thing is to marinate the bird for at least 2-3 days. The powerful taste of Sichuan peppercorns and the long marinating time will do most of the flavoring job. This is a banquet dish, as well as a holiday favorite.

3 tablespoons Sichuan peppercorns
1 (4~5 pounds) young duckling, thoroughly thawed
1 tablespoon salt
1 teaspoon pepper
2 tablespoons flour for coating
leafy greens or onion for garnish

Method

1. Heat a pan or wok over medium heat without adding any oil. Pour in the Sichuan peppercorns and stir briskly until color changes slightly, about 30 seconds. Turn off the heat and let cool.

2. Trim excess fat from the duckling and drain well. Place the duckling in a pan or any container where you can easily work on the bird. First, sprinkle the salt all over the duckling then sprinkle evenly with the pepper. Then press the peppercorns on all parts of the duckling, especially the inside, until it is covered with brown spots of peppercorns. When this is done, place the duckling in a plastic food storage bag and leave it in the refrigerator to marinate for at least 2 days.

3. When ready to cook, wash the duckling under running water until the peppercorns are gone. Drain well and pat dry with a paper towel. Place the duckling in a baking pan and bake at 350°F for 40~50 minutes. Let cool to room temperature before frying. Dust a thin layer of flour all over the skin of the duckling.

4. In a wok, heat 1 cup of oil over medium-high heat until very hot. Carefully lower the duckling into the oil and let it fry for at least 3 minutes or until golden brown. Use the lid as a shield when you turn the bird over since it might splatter. Using a pair of tongs, slowly turn the duck over and allow it to fry evenly. When the duckling is nicely browned on all sides, remove to drain on a rack and then absorb excess oil with a paper towel. Let it cool slightly. Then cut into halves or 1-inch strips and arrange neatly on a serving platter. Garnish with onion or leafy green. Serve immediately.

6~8 servings

SEAFOOD: DELICACIES FROM THE WATER

The Chinese are perhaps the greatest seafood eaters in the world. In any Chinatown you are likely to find streets lined with seafood restaurants and fish stands. And in almost any Chinese restaurant you visit in the United States, you are likely to find a large selection of seafood dishes. This passion of the Chinese for fish dates back centuries ago when meats were scarce in China but fish was plentiful. The ancient Chinese savored fish for its delicat quality, while today we see its healthy benefit as well. Interesting evidence can be found in the Chinese written language. The Chinese character "鮮," which means fresh and delicate, is composed of two parts: The ideogram for fish, 魚," appears on the left and the word for lamb, "羊," is on the right. Apparently, these two animals were highly prized foods in ancient China. Ironically, although fish is still a national obsession, lamb has lost its popularity to other meats.

Seafood may be a much sought-after delicacy, yet making an outstanding seafood dish demands a great deal of skill and a considerable amount of time; therefore, not many home cooks are willing to tackle such a challenging job. As a result, seafood cuisine has become the specialty of many restaurants. For the average Chinese household, dining out often means having a seafood dinner, not only because restaurants offer professional cooking standards, but because they have access to a greater variety of fresh seafood. If you like to try authentic Chinese seafood, your best bet would be a good Chinese restaurant patronized by the Chinese.

In Chinese restaurants, seafood is cooked in a totally different way from Western-style seafood. If you like a strong taste, you might want to try the Sichuan (or Hunan) chili bean fish, sweet and sour crispy-skin fish, or the famous Shanghai smoked fish. Chinese smoked fish does not taste smoky at all; it has a nice crusty five-spice flavor and is extremely tasty. People who prefer a lighter taste should try steamed fish, Cantonese seafood casseroles or seafood stir-fries. Shrimp lovers will probably enjoy the unique and elegant salt-roasted shrimp, which has an aromatic light taste and a crispy texture, unlike the Western heavily breaded shrimp, which tends to be too oily. You can find the best seafood dishes at good Cantonese seafood restaurants where they serve seafood in the most delicious and creative ways.

Chinese home cooks treat fish in much the same way as they handle meat, with marinating being an essential step toward good cooking. There are many ways to prepare seafood, but I have limited my discussion on seafood cooking to only the following techniques, as these are the most common and effective methods.

Steaming: The purpose of this method is to preserve the pure taste and the shape of the fish. It is paramount to look for fresh fish with a mild and tender taste, such as sea bass, flounder, gray sole and cod. Both whole fish and fillets may be used, but first marinate them with salt and wine briefly before adding other seasonings. The following toppings will enhance the natural taste of fish: ginger, scallions, dried Chinese mushrooms, ham, black beans, hot peppers and Chinese pickled vegetables.

Shallow-Frying: This is the first step to many elaborate fish dishes. The advantage of this method is that most of the fishy taste can be eliminated during frying. However, the common problem of frying fish is how to keep the fish skin intact to preserve its shape and flavor. This, of course, requires some skill and experience.

Here are some rules for beginners:

* Select a firm textured whole fish for frying; red snapper, flounder, sea bass and porgie are suitable for this cooking method. Before frying, the fish must be marinated and drained well.
* Add enough oil to fry, at least 1/3 cup. Once the fish is in hot oil, do not touch it for the first 2 minutes. This is to allow the skin to form a light crust. When the bottom is nicely browned, gently flip to the other side and continue to fry until light brown.
* Another way to prevent the skin from falling apart is to dust the skin with a little flour before frying.

Stir-Frying : Stir-fried fish fillets taste smooth and flavorful. Unfortunately, most fish disintegrate during the course of stir-frying. Try using firmer fish, such as catfish, orange roughy and ocean perch, which can withstand the tossing and turning. Cut them into thick slices and marinate briefly before cooking. They taste best when stir-fried with just shredded ginger, scallions or with seasonal vegetables. As for shellfish, no other cooking method suits them better than stir-frying. High heat and hot oil intensify the flavors of shrimp, squid and scallops while preserving their texture, which might otherwise toughen from long cooking.

Besides being consumed as a main dish, fish and shellfish are often used in Chinese kitchens as seasonings in sauces and fillings. If you have tasted shrimp-filled dumplings and dim sum, you will marvel at this ingenious creation. The shrimp not only tastes astonishingly delicious inside the filling but it also imparts a distinctive flavor to the pastry. The use of shrimp does not end here. It is used widely with ground pork to fill wontons, tofu, egg omelets, mushrooms, green bell peppers and many other dishes. Shrimp fillings indeed add an elegant taste to food.

To make things easier for busy cooks, some Chinese food factories produce a ready-to-use fish paste that tastes just as good as freshly chopped shrimp filling. This is a well-seasoned mixed fish paste that comes in an 8-ounce plastic container and is sold in most Chinese food stores. I have read in Chinese food columns that many home cooks wholeheartedly embrace this product. It is convenient, inexpensive and very versatile. Besides using it as an all-purpose filling, you can count on it to enhance your soups, stews and stir-fried dishes.

My mission in teaching you about Chinese seafood would not be complete if I fail to share with you the shopping experience of Chinese home cooks. A high demand for freshness and variety has led many Chinese to travel to Chinatown for seafood supplies. If you have ever walked around the fish markets in New York City or San Francisco and seen live fish swimming in the tanks, crabs crawling in the baskets and freshly killed fish with their tails still moving, you would perhaps understand why some Chinese drive for hours just to find these beauties. On top of freshness, the prices at these fish markets are irresistibly low compared to prices in most supermarkets. Even Western tourists are drawn to these fish stands, gleefully purchasing lobsters that are much more costly elsewhere. This is how these shoppers keep their seafood fresh: they put an ice chest in the car. They also purchase a few weeks' supply so that it is worth the trip.

In the last decade, many Chinese markets have opened in suburban areas and they seem to have diverted some of the shopping traffic from Chinatown to the suburbs. The proximity of these markets saves the residents many trips to Chinatown. Some of these rural Chinese food stores that are located in malls are as large as supermarkets. What is remarkable about these stores is that they have brought a small part of the seafood stands from Chinatown to the suburbs. Prices in suburban markets may be slightly higher than in Chinatown, but the freshness and the selection are similar. I hope people who love seafood will benefit from these suburban markets.

青椒炒魚球

Stir-Fried Catfish with Green Bell Peppers

With a tender texture and mild taste, catfish is excellent for stir-frying. In this recipe, catfish and the fragrant green bell peppers complement each other well in a light sauce.

3/4 pound catfish or any firm
   white fish
1 large green bell pepper
1 small red chili pepper
2 teaspoons fermented black
   beans
oil for stir-frying
2 tablespoons chopped garlic,
   divided
salt and pepper to taste

Marinade
2 teaspoons dry sherry
2 teaspoons cornstarch
salt and pepper to taste

Seasoning Sauce
4 tablespoons chicken broth
1 tablespoon oyster sauce

Method
1. Cut the catfish into 1/2-inch squares. Place it in the marinade for 30 minutes or longer. Rinse the green bell pepper and red chili pepper. Cut the green bell pepper into 1/2-inch squares and the red chili pepper into slices. Soak the fermented black beans in cold water for 2 minutes; rinse lightly and drain.

2. Heat 3 tablespoons of oil until very hot. Sizzle half the garlic. Immediately pour in the green bell pepper, red chili peppers and the fermented black beans. Sprinkle salt to taste, tossing gently to coat with oil and heat. Cook for 1~2 minutes then remove. Clean the wok with a paper towel.

3. Heat 5 tablespoons of oil over high heat. Sizzle the rest of the garlic. Stir-fry the catfish until the color changes completely. Return the green bell peppers to the wok and add the seasoning sauce (sprinkle salt and pepper to taste). Stir to mix flavors together. Cook for another minute or two. Remove and serve immediately.

4~6 servings

香煎沙文魚
Sautéed Salmon Steak

Although not a fish indigenous to China, salmon, with its beautiful bright color and rich taste, is becoming a highly regarded seafood in many Chinese kitchens. In this recipe, salmon steak is first marinated with a special sauce, then sautéed until crusty. Adding a light onion sauce will give it an excellent finishing touch.

1 pound salmon steaks
4~6 slices paper thin ginger
oil for sautéing
salt and pepper to taste
  herbs (cilantro, basil or
  scallions) for garnish

Marinade
2 tablespoons rice wine or
  dry sherry
1 teaspoon soy sauce
1 tablespoon sha cha sauce
  or Chinese barbecue sauce
  (optional)
pepper to taste

Garnishing Sauce
1 teaspoon chopped garlic
2~3 wedges onion
1/3 cup chicken broth
2 teaspoons oyster sauce

Method
1. Rinse the salmon lightly
   and drain well. Rub both
   sides of the salmon with
   the ginger slices and then
   immerse in the marinade.
   Let sit for at least 20
   minutes or longer. Drain
   thoroughly before cooking;
   save the marinade for the
   garnishing sauce.

2. In a flat pan, heat 3
   tablespoons of oil over
   medium-high heat. Lower
   the fish into the pan and
   allow it to brown slowly for
   2~3 minutes. Turn the fish
   over before the color
   becomes too dark. Brown
   the other side for 3
   minutes, then lower the
   heat and cover with a lid.
   Allow to brown slowly for
   about 8~10 minutes or
   until a crust is formed.
   Remove to a serving plate.

3. To make the garnishing
   sauce: In another pan,
   heat 1 tablespoon of oil
   and lightly brown the
   garlic and onion. Add the
   chicken broth, oyster sauce
   and the leftover marinade.
   Simmer over low heat to
   blend the flavors well,
   about 2 minutes. Remove
   and pour over the fish.
   Garnish with the herbs
   and serve immediately.

2~4 servings

Note
Look for very fresh salmon steak that is deep orange in color. Ask the vendor to remove the scales for you.

清蒸魚
Steamed Striped Bass

Steaming is the best way to cook fish. It retains the natural sweetness and tenderness of the fish while preserving its delicate taste. This is also a very adaptable dish. You can make it more elaborate by following this recipe, or if you wish to keep it simple, leave out the ham and the fish will still be tasty. If striped bass is unavailable, substitute sea bass, flounder or other mild-tasting fish.

1 whole striped bass or any
   mild taste fish, about 1 1/4
   pounds
oil for sautéing

Marinade
1 teaspoon salt
1 tablespoon dry sherry

Seasonings
2 tablespoons shredded
   Canadian bacon
1/2 tablespoon shredded
   ginger
2 tablespoon shredded
   scallions, white part only

Method
1. Score the fish diagonally, twice on each side. This will allow the fish to absorb flavors faster. Marinate with salt and sherry for 10 minutes. Place the fish in a deep plate and spread the seasonings evenly over the fish (use half of the scallions).

2. Steam the fish over medium-high heat for about 8~10 minutes. Remove the fish from the steamer and replace the wilted scallions with fresh ones (save a few pieces for sauteing). Heat 1 1/2 tablespoons oil and sauté the remaining pieces of scallion (white part) until light brown. Pour the hot oil over the fish. Pouring hot oil over the steamed fish gives extra aroma to the dish. Serve immediately.

4 servings

紅燒紅魚
Braised Red Snapper

Well-cooked Chinese braised fish is a treat, but most of these dishes require an enormous amount of skill and effort to prepare. My sister-in-law gave me this recipe, which is less complex and easier to make. Sautéing brings aroma to the fish and simmering with sauce adds an extra richness. Serve this dish as a main course with rice.

1 whole red snapper, about 1 1/2 pounds
salt for seasoning fish
flour for dusting
oil for frying
1 large scallion stalk
6 slices ginger

Seasoning Sauce

1/4 cup rice wine or dry sherry
1/4 cup sugar
1/4 cup vinegar
2 tablespoons soy sauce
1/3 cup chicken broth (or water)

Method

1. Clean and rinse the fish thoroughly; drain well. Sprinkle salt lightly on both sides of the fish. Let stand for at least 10 minutes. Drain again and pat dry with a paper towel. Dust a little flour lightly over the fish. This will prevent the skin from falling off.

2. Heat the wok until very hot. Add 1/4 cup of oil and swirl the wok to coat with the oil. Carefully slip the fish into the hot oil from the side of the wok to avoid splattering. Sauté over high heat until light brown. Flip over and brown the other side.

3. Add the seasoning sauce, scallions and ginger. Cover and simmer for about 5 minutes over medium heat, basting occasionally. Add water if needed.

4. When the sauce has been reduced to about 1/3 of a cup, it is ready to serve. Remove and serve hot.

4~6 servings

Note

Heating the wok first before adding the oil is a crucial step in sautéing fish. It prevents the fish from sticking to the wok.

蔥薑炒蝦

Quick-Fried Ginger Scallion Shrimp

Shrimp is a delicacy that needs no sauce to enhance its flavor. In this dish, its wonderful taste is brought to perfection by the ginger and scallions. By not removing the shells you preserve the tenderness. If you don't like shells, remove them but remember to shorten the cooking time so that the shrimp will not get too chewy.

1 1/4 pounds fresh medium
   shrimp
2 tablespoon dry sherry
salt to taste
3 tablespoons shredded
   ginger
3 stalks scallions
oil for stir-frying

Method

1. Rinse and drain the shrimp. Using a pair of kitchen scissors, cut off the legs and tails. Then devein by cutting the top shell open. Marinate the shrimp with sherry, salt and ginger for 30 minutes or longer. Drain well before cooking.

2. Rinse the scallions lightly and shake off the water. Flatten the stalks of the scallions by pounding both the stems and the leaves with the large side of a cleaver or a heavy kitchen knife. Cut the flattened scallions into diagonal strips.

3. Heat 4 tablespoons of oil over high heat. Sizzle 3 pieces of scallion stems until light brown. Add the shrimp immediately, stirring constantly to coat with oil and heat. When the color of the shrimp begins to change, add the remaining scallions. Continue turning and mixing until the shrimp have turned completely pink. Remove. Serve hot or cold.

4~6 servings

鹽酥蝦
Sautéed Shrimp

This is an incredibly tasty dish. Even if you can't follow the recipe exactly, it will still be finger-licking good. The reason is simple: shrimp is the most flavorful seafood when fresh. Deep-frying and sautéing intensify the taste and add crispness, making it a scrumptious dish for any occasion.

1 pound medium shrimp
2 teaspoons dry sherry
2 teaspoons cornstarch
oil for sautéing
1/2 teaspoon salt
pepper to taste
1/4 teaspoon five-spice
    powder

Method

1. Do not peel the shrimp. Rinse the shrimp and devein by making a cut halfway down the back of the shrimp. Marinate with the sherry for 10~15 minutes or longer. Drain thoroughly and pat dry with a paper towel. Add the cornstarch and mix well before deep-frying.

2. Heat 1 cup of oil over high heat. Deep-fry the shrimp in 2 batches until the color changes and a crust is formed. Remove the oil to a bowl. Clean the wok with a paper towel.

3. Reheat the wok without adding any oil. Return the shrimp to the wok, stirring briskly over medium-low heat for about 2 minutes. Add the salt, pepper and five-spice powder; mix well and serve immediately.

2~6 servings

魚吐司
Fish Toast

Fish toast is a variation of the famous dim sum "Shrimp Toast" and is extremely tasty. Since frozen fish paste is fully seasoned, it is almost a ready-made filling, making this favorite dish simple and less laborious. If you are too far from a Chinese market, substitute chopped shrimp.

8 slices white bread
1 pound container fish paste
oil for deep-frying

Seasonings
3 tablespoons minced water
  chestnuts
2 tablespoons minced celery
2 teaspoons sesame oil
2 tablespoons cornstarch

Method
1. Bake the white bread at 300°F for 15~20 minutes or until light brown and crusty. Toasting the bread prevents it from soaking up excess oil during frying.

2. Thoroughly mix the fish paste with the seasonings. Cut each piece of toast into 4 triangles. Spread approximately 2 teaspoons of fish mixture on each triangle to form a smooth mound. A small amount of filling is easier to work with than a larger amount. Fill all the triangles. If there is any filling left, use it in soups.

3. Heat 2 cups of oil until very hot. Stick the end of a chopstick in oil. If bubbles appear, it is ready to fry. Deep-fry fish toast in small batches, about 6~8 pieces at a time, until both sides turn light brown. Remove with a slotted spoon, using paper towels to absorb excess oil. Serve immediately.

Makes 32 pieces

干貝蘿蔔球

Braised Scallops with Daikon

Scallops are an ideal choice when entertaining, but one needs to use special care to retain their tender texture. With the support of daikon, ginger and chicken broth, this delicacy is brought to perfection. For entertaining, follow this recipe closely; but for family meals, you can simply cut the vegetables into chunks.

3/4 pound medium scallops
1 tablespoon baking soda
  mixed with 1 cup water
1 large daikon, about 2
  pounds
2 medium carrots (try to buy
  fat ones)
oil for stir-frying
2 tablespoons chopped
  scallion, white part only

Marinade
1 1/2 teaspoons dry sherry
1/2 teaspoon salt

Seasoning Sauce
1 teaspoon sugar
2/3 cup chicken broth
salt and pepper to taste

Cornstarch Mixture
1 tablespoon cornstarch
2 tablespoons water

Method

1. Soak the scallops in the baking soda solution for about 15 minutes. This prevents the scallops from toughening. Rinse out the baking soda and drain well. Place the scallops in the marinade for at least 20 minutes. Then pour onto a strainer to drain thoroughly; set aside.

2. Peel the daikon and the carrots. Place them in a medium-sized pot with water to cover. Boil for about 30 minutes or until tender. Remove and let cool to room temperature. Use a melon-baller to scoop out daikon and carrot balls for a more attractive look. Trim irregular parts with a knife.

3. Heat 3 tablespoons of oil. Sizzle half of the scallions until fragrant. Add the scallops and stir-fry until the color changes. Remove and set aside. Wash the wok clean and dry with a paper towel.

4. Heat 2 tablespoons oil and sizzle the rest of the scallions briefly. Add the daikon balls and carrot balls; stir and turn to coat with flavors, about 2~3 minutes. Add the scallops and the seasoning sauce. Cover and simmer for 2 minutes. Thicken with the cornstarch mixture before removing to a serving bowl. Serve hot.

4~6 servings

海鮮煲
Seafood Hot Pot

This is a half-soup and half-stew dish, one of the very elaborate seafood recipes frequently ordered by Chinese diners in a Chinese restaurant. Technically, this is a combination of browning and stewing. And the dish is made elegant by the marriage of an array of colorful ingredients with an aromatic sauce.

2 sea bass steaks, 4~6 ounces each
1/2 pound medium shrimp (must be very fresh)
oil for sautéing
8~10 fish balls
1/3 pound clams
1/2 pound fresh mushrooms
6 stalks baby bok choy
1 package medium-firm tofu
2 slices ginger
2 stalks scallions
2 cups chicken broth

Marinade
2 tablespoons dry sherry, divided
1 teaspoon salt, divided

Dipping Sauce
1 tablespoon oyster sauce
2 teaspoons sha cha sauce
2 tablespoons soy sauce
3 tablespoons chicken broth

Method
1. Rinse the sea bass steaks and shrimp (devein if needed) well. Marinate the sea bass steaks briefly with half of the marinade ingredients. Use the remaining half to flavor the shrimp briefly. In a pan, lightly brown the sea bass steaks with 2 tablespoons of oil and set aside.

2. Rinse the fish balls, clams, mushrooms and bok choy separately. Cut the tofu into chunks.

3. In another pan, heat 1 tablespoon of oil and lightly brown the ginger and scallion stems. Add the clams and chicken broth and cook for 5 minutes to extract flavor. This is your flavorful soup base for the hot pot.

4. In a large heatproof glassware or a stewing pot, arrange the seafood, vegetables and tofu nicely. Add the soup and cook for about 3~5 minutes to heat through and blend the flavors. Serve with the dipping sauce

6 servings

Note
You can use any type of fresh mushrooms available — shitake mushrooms, straw mushrooms, button mushrooms, or oyster mushrooms. Use the canned varieties if fresh mushrooms are not available.

PASTRIES AND DESSERTS : Reinventing Chinese Sweets

Chinese restaurants rarely serve desserts and this seem to have misled many Westerners into thinking that the Chinese don't eat desserts at all, or that they have a very limited pastry repertoire. Even some native Chinese food authorities have spoken negatively about Chinese pastries. But as a Chinese home cook and food writer who has been active in food circles, I hold a significantly different view of Chinese sweets. This could due to my childhood experiences with Chinese sweets, my reading of food articles written in Chinese and my recent interviews with several Chinese pastry chefs who are masters in the art of Chinese pastries. It is true that Chinese pastries do not look as fancy as their Western counterparts and that they come in fewer varieties as compared to the wide range of Chinese dim sum snacks. But Chinese sweets are by no means inferior as perceived by many people. They are, in fact, the lost art of an ancient food culture.

To understand why very few Chinese restaurants serve desserts, we must go back in history and look at the cultural tradition of the Chinese. Unlike most Westerners who eat desserts as part of their meal, the ancient Chinese used pastries only for special occasions. In those days, well-made cakes and pastries were luxuries that commoners could not afford. Thus, they were eaten only during special holidays and festivals, such as Chinese New Year, Dragon Boat Festival and Moon Festival. Cakes were served on weddings to symbolize happiness for the newly-weds. Steamed buns shaped likes peaches were served on birthdays to signify longevity. Certainly, there were other types of sweets for common people. For example, homemade sweet soups were used for health reasons—to strengthen the immune system or to heal certain minor ailments. These health soups taste so good that even to this day people still enjoy drinking them as beverages.

Few people know that fancy elaborate cakes and other sophisticated pastries did exist in ancient China. Why some of these treasures have become extinct or are virtually unknown to food enthusiasts remains a puzzle. To solve this puzzle, we should delve into the culinary history of Chinese sweets. In ancient China, Chinese chefs did not attend formal training classes but learned their craft strictly by working their way up through apprenticeships in pastry shops. Some recipes, which were closely guarded family secrets, perished when there were no descendants to carry on the trade. There were many dark periods in Chinese history when wars devastated the country and left the people impoverished. The pastry industry was inevitably disrupted and many great recipes lost. During the last century, Western-style sweets began to emerge and took over a large share of the confectionery business in China, which inevitably affected the growth of traditional pastries industry.

But it is heartening to know that some dedicated pastry chefs in China are now trying to revive the ancient art of pastry making. In the summer of 1998, I had the privilege of visiting one of the top pastry shops in Taiwan— The Original Sun Bakery of Taizhong (Taichung) City.

The shop is famous for its "sun cake," a crisp flaky cake with wonderful gel-like filling. But I fell in love with another specialty—the "engagement cake," which has a very subtle aroma and a texture that has no equal and a sensational tenderness that melts right in your mouth. According to the owner, this cake is made with a very special process: first the rice flour is steamed, then mixed with spices and molded into beautiful round cakes.

While in Taipei, I found another pastry shop (which is Shanghai-style) located near the famous "South Gate Market." The store looked small and obscure, but the variety of traditional pastries was truly impressive and the taste was surprisingly outstanding. I spoke to the owner Mr. Liu and told him that discovering his store was a reward for my long search for great Chinese pastries. By pure luck, within two days, I was brought to another unique eatery—King Join (Administrator of Emperor City). This is a chain café selling ancient palace food that was enjoyed by the Empress of the Qing Dynasty (1835~1908). What a unique idea! The name and decor

alone were a great attraction, not to mention the sophisticated tasting soft cakes served. After taking a bite into one of those delectable soft cakes, I could understand why they are tremendously popular with the Taiwanese. I suggested to its PR Director, I-Rue Chen, that the King Join chain should open similar stores in America and in other places to let the world taste the best of Chinese desserts.

It is certainly too far to go to China for a taste of desserts, unless your travel plans or business bring you there. But with the proliferation of Chinese specialty food stores in this country, you might be able to find some Chinese sweets and pastries that please your palate. Here are some guidelines that might be helpful if you are truly serious about getting a taste of Chinese sweets.

Cantonese-Style Sweets
Cantonese-style sweets have the longest presence in America because the earlier Chinese immigrants to America were mainly from the province of Guangdong in China. You can find these sweets in Chinatown bakeries, dim sum houses and sweet cafés. The specialties from these outlets

include: almond cookies, honey noodle cakes, sesame balls, assorted nut moon cake, winter melon flaky cake, steamed yellow cake, white sugar rice soft cake, water chestnut soft cake and all kinds of custard cups. Cantonese cuisine is also known for its great tasting sweet soups. Among the best are creamy red bean soup, creamy mung bean soup, creamy sesame soup and sweet rice ball soup.

Shanghai-Style Sweets
This group of sweets has a marvelous variety of flaky cakes that are perhaps more delicious and sophisticated than that of other regions in China. Although new in this country, Shanghai-style sweets are quickly gaining popularity. You can find packaged Shanghai flaky cakes or moon cakes in large Chinese food markets or specialty stores. But eating crispy flaky bean cakes fresh out of the oven in a Shanghai restaurant is a most enjoyable culinary experience.

Taiwanese-Style Sweets
This is another new addition to Chinatown bakery shops in this country. Their most famous products are flaky sun cakes, fruit-filled cookies, sweet rice soft cakes

and also their famous engagement cakes.

Northern-Style Sweets

Beijing sweets include an interesting array of palace desserts. Unfortunately, chefs who make Northern-style sweets are hard to find in areas outside of China. But if you can locate a Chinese restaurant where they sell fresh bean milk, you will have a great chance of tasting the absolutely delicious and crispy oven-baked sweet flat bread!

Festival Cakes and National Favorites

Chinese festival cakes bear special symbolic meanings. For instance, the Chinese eat New Year's cake to symbolize prosperity. During the autumn harvest Moon Festival, moon cakes are used to signify reunion and loving relationship between family members. Other favorite desserts such as Eight-Jeweled Rice Pudding and Taro Pudding are usually served at wedding banquets.

Living in the United States is like living in a global kitchen with a stunning diversity of foods and a wonderful array of ingredients from every corner of the world. This is definitely a haven for creative cooks, who use a combination of ingredients from different countries and techniques from different cuisines, to create a new class of cuisine — fusion cuisine, or nouvelle cuisine. Fusion cuisine is not new in China if we were to look at the innovative sweets that Cantonese chefs have invented in the last few decades. Western influence is obvious in Cantonese-style confectioneries such as sweet breads, turnovers and custard tarts, which are the hot favorites in Chinese bakeries.

Over a decade ago, I began to discover the pleasure of using Western spices in Chinese pastries. I was especially fond of using cinnamon powder, coffee, condensed milk or ice-cream toppings to flavor Chinese pastry fillings. Adding a touch of these new flavors truly brings life to many century-old Chinese pastries, making them much more appealing. My happy experiments resulted in a beautiful dessert book. Subsequently I went on to write many other fusion dessert recipes, a few of which I have included in this chapter.

I hope to generate new interest in Chinese sweets through this cookbook in which I share my experience in creating and making Chinese sweets. I have also discussed my conviction with some Chinese pastry chefs, hoping to bring new enthusiasm to a fading industry. I was elated when I found out that Spencer Chen, the owner of Sweet and Tart Café in New York's Chinatown, is also an avid advocate of reinventing Chinese sweets through creation of new recipes.

Chinese chefs are indeed masters of filled pastries and delicate soft cakes. By combining ancient Chinese pastry skills with Western ingredients and techniques, there could be endless possibilities in pastry making. If more people were interested in reviving the industry, then Chinese traditional pastries could be upgraded to a higher standard, which could then be enjoyed by Westerners, just as dim sum is. There is no reason why this great culinary art should suffer a decline in popularity.

粟子年糕
Rice Cake with Chestnut Paste

This is an improvised version of the classic rice cake. The nice part of the recipe is that there is no sifting of flour and beating of eggs. The cake has a uniquely smooth texture, which is the result of using the bean paste and chestnut puree. If you like a more dramatic taste, cut the cake into 1-inch cubes, dip the cubes in an egg-and-flour batter then deep-fry until crusty.

1 (1-pound) can red bean paste
1 cup chestnut paste
1 (15-ounce) can evaporated milk
1/2 stick butter or margarine
1 cup sugar
1/2 cup butterscotch ice cream topping for flavoring
1 cup water
1 cup sticky rice flour
1 cup regular rice flour
candied chestnuts or dried fruits for garnish
2 (8-inch) pie pans

Method

1. In a large mixing bowl, blend the bean paste, chestnut paste, evaporated milk, butter, sugar, butterscotch topping and water together. Gradually add the sticky rice flour and regular rice flour, half a cup at a time, mixing gently until well blended and smooth.

2. Grease 2 pie pans with oil and pour the mixture onto the pans. Using the candied chestnut, make a design on top of the cake mixture and steam over medium-high heat for 30~40 minutes. Remove and let cool. Serve at room temperature. For an impressive taste, cut the cake into thick slices and sauté both sides until light brown. Refrigerate leftovers.

Makes 2 cakes

Note

Chestnut paste is available at gourmet food stores and some supermarkets. Sticky rice flour may be purchased from a health food store or a Chinese food store.

八寶飯

Eight-Jeweled Rice Pudding

This classic dessert is served at all Chinese banquets, not only because it has a lucky name, but also because it looks attractive and tastes marvelous. Except in a few Chinese pastry stores, it is hard to find this unique rice pudding. In fact, this is a very simple dish. You can make a few dishes at one time and freeze them. Whenever you need a great dessert for a party, simply steam the rice pudding for 20~30 minutes or until soft. (Never serve this dish cold.) It will make your family and friends very happy.

1 1/4 cup sticky rice
1 1/4 cup water
1 tablespoon butter
2 tablespoons sugar
2 large pieces candied
   papaya
1/4 cup raisins
1/3 cup sweet canned lotus
   seeds or candied cherries
1/2 (1-pound) can red bean
   paste

Almond Sauce

2/3 cup water
1 teaspoon almond extract
2 tablespoons sugar
1 tablespoon cornstarch
dissolved in 2 tablespoons
   water

Method

1. Soak the sticky rice in 1
   1/4 cup of water for about
   30 minutes. Steam the rice
   over high heat for 30~40
   minutes. If the rice is not
   completely cooked,
   sprinkle a little water and
   cook a few more minutes
   (5~10). Remove the rice
   from the steamer and mix
   in the butter and sugar
   while hot.

2. Lightly grease a medium
   mixing bowl. Use cookie
   cutters to cut the candied
   papaya into heart shapes
   (or other shapes). Then
   arrange these shapes
   (combining them with
   raisins, lotus seeds or a
   few other candied fruits)
   into your own designs on
   the bottom of the bowl. On
   top of this design, cover
   with a thin layer of
   steamed rice. Smooth out
   evenly with a serving
   spoon (or clean hands).
   Next spread the red bean
   paste on top of the rice.
   Lastly, add another layer
   of sticky rice on top and
   smooth out with a spoon or
   your clean hand. Steam
   the rice pudding for 15~25
   minutes over medium-high
   heat.

3. In the meantime, cook the
   almond sauce ingredients
   over low heat until
   smooth. If you want to
   skip this step, you may use
   maple syrup instead.
   When ready to serve,
   invert the rice pudding on
   a serving platter. Now you
   can see the beautiful
   design of the pudding.
   Pour the almond sauce on
   top and serve hot.

4 servings

Note

**Sticky rice is available
in Chinese stores and
health food stores.**

甜春卷
Sweet Spring Rolls

Sweet Spring Rolls may be a novelty in this country, but they are popular in certain parts of China, such as Shanghai and Suzhou. In this recipe, sticky rice and red bean paste contribute their best assets to the Spring Rolls — the soft and resilient texture of sticky rice contrasts wonderfully with the smooth taste of red bean paste. There are endless ways of using spring roll skins. For the adventurous cook, you might want to try wrapping your favorite pudding or pie filling in Spring Roll

2 cups short grain sticky rice
2 cups water
1 tablespoon butter
1/3 cup sugar
1 (1-pound) can red bean paste
2/3 teaspoon cinnamon powder
1 package (25-30 pieces) imported thin Spring Roll wrappers
1 egg, beaten
2 cups oil for deep-frying

Method

1. In a mixing bowl, soak the sticky rice in 2 cups of cold water for about 30 minutes. Steam the rice, with the water, over high heat for about 30 minutes or until translucent. If the rice is not completely cooked, sprinkle 2 tablespoons of water and continue to steam for another 10 minutes. Remove the cooked rice from the steamer. Fluff and break the grains loose with a fork. Add the butter and sugar, mixing thoroughly with a clean hand.

2. For a richer-tasting red bean paste, mix the cinnamon powder with the red bean paste.

3. To assemble: Set up an assembly line on the kitchen table. Place a wrapper in front of you. Put about 2 tablespoons of rice near the corner closest to you. Shape the rice into a 1 by 3-inch sausage. On top of the rice add about 1 1/3 tablespoons of red bean paste, shaping into the same size. Wrap filling tightly as though wrapping a package. Seal with beaten egg. Repeat with the rest of filling.

4. Since fried Spring Rolls must be eaten on the same day for best results, fry just enough for your family and guests; refrigerate the rest for future use. Heat 2 cups of oil over medium-high heat and deep-fry Spring Rolls in batches until golden brown. Serve while it is still crispy.

Makes 25 rolls

什錦甜酒羹
Deluxe Rice Wine Dessert

This is a modern version of the classic sweet soup — a favorite dessert in China. It looks absolutely fabulous with the colorful combination of white, orange, yellow and red. The smooth, soothing and lively taste serves as a perfect conclusion to a delicious meal. If you are too far from a Chinese market to buy rice wine sauce, substitute amaretto.

1 (11-ounce) can Mandarin
   oranges
4-6 medium strawberries or
   red cherries, cut into
   smaller pieces

Egg Custard Mixture
3 medium eggs
2 tablespoons cornstarch
2 tablespoons sugar
1/2 cup water
1/2 teaspoon almond extract

Rice Wine Soup
1 1/2 cup sweet rice wine
   sauce (use mostly the
   rice)
3 cups water
3/4 cup sugar

Method
1. To make the egg custard:
   Beat the eggs until frothy.

In another bowl, dissolve the cornstarch and sugar in water. Add the almond extract and combine the mixture with the beaten eggs, mixing well. Grease an 8-inch pie pan or any dish of a similar size and shape. Pour the egg mixture onto the pan and steam over medium heat for about 12~15 minutes or until firm. Allow it to cool completely, then cut into 1/2-inch squares or diamond shapes.

2. To make the rice wine soup: In a medium-sized saucepan, bring the rice wine sauce, water and sugar to a gentle boil. Simmer over medium heat for two minutes, then turn off the heat and allow it to cool completely.

3. To serve: In a large serving bowl, combine the rice wine soup, egg custard, Mandarin oranges and strawberries. Chill and serve cold.

6~8 servings

Note
Use only sweet rice wine sauce bought from Chinese stores. Cut the strawberries into smaller pieces so they will float to the top of the finished dish.

芝果杏仁凍
Almond-Mango Jello Delight

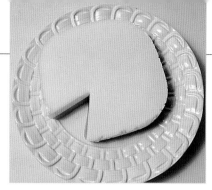

The Chinese have always been fans of soft cakes made from rice, wheat or beans. Here's another new favorite—soft gelatin cake. This is much more sophisticated than the gelatin desserts sold at supermarkets. It is soft but not watery, light but with a fruity, refreshing taste that will delight both Chinese and Westerners.

2 medium ripe mangoes
1 1/4 cups sugar
4 packages unflavored
   gelatin
1 cup milk
1 teaspoon almond extract

Method

1. Peel the mangoes, cut into large pieces and purée with a food processor. Line a large square heat-proof glassware dish with plastic wrap. This will make removing the cake easier.

2. In a saucepan, bring 1/2 cup of water and 1/2 cup of sugar to a gentle boil. Dissolve 2 packages of the gelatin in 1/3 cup of water and add to the boiling sugar solution, mixing quickly to break any lumps. Once thoroughly blended, turn off the heat. Allow the liquid to cool slightly, then add the mango purée. Mix well and pour into the lined heatproof glassware. Chill for about 40 minutes or until congealed.

3. Wash the saucepan well. Bring 2/3 cup of water and 3/4 cup of sugar to a gentle boil. Dissolve 2 packages of the gelatin in 1/3 cup of water and add to the boiling sugar solution. Mix well and turn off the heat. Add the milk and almond extract to the gelatin mixture, stirring to mix well. To cool quickly, sit the pan in ice water and stir with a spoon. Pour the almond milk mixture over the congealed mango gelatin and chill for another 45 minutes or until set.

4. When ready to serve, lift the whole cake out of the container. Cut into squares or diamond shapes. Leftovers may be kept for about a week in the refrigerator.

Makes 1 soft cake

紫露麻球

Sesame Balls in Creamy Sauce

These sesame balls are irresistible. They are the best sellers in dim sum houses and Chinese markets. This is an adapted recipe that gives the original one added color and another dimension of taste. Taro, the fragrant Chinese potato, is a very popular ingredient in Chinese desserts. If it is unavailable in your area, try yucca, which is quite close to taro in taste and texture.

1 cup white sesame seeds
2 cups oil for deep-frying

Taro Sauce
1 small taro, the size of a
  small papaya
2/3 cup sugar
1/3 cup cornstarch mixed
  with 2/3 cup water

Dough
1 medium sweet potato
  (about 3~4 ounces)
2 cups sticky rice flour
1/2 cup water, approximately
  (depending on the size of
  the sweet potato)

Filling
1 (1-pound) can red bean
  paste
1 teaspoon cinnamon powder
  (optional)

Method
1. To make the taro sauce:
   Peel the brown skin of the
   taro and cut into thin
   slices. Place the taro slices
   in a medium pot and add
   water to cover, about 3
   inches above. Boil over
   medium-high heat until
   very tender, about 30~50
   minutes (depending on the
   freshness of taro bought).
   Mash the taro pieces into
   paste over low heat. Add

water as needed. Then add
the sugar and cornstarch
solution, mixing well to
turn it into a creamy
mixture.

2. To make the dough: Peel
   the sweet potato and cut
   into quarters. Cook the
   sweet potato pieces in a
   small amount of water
   until very tender, about 20
   minutes. In a mixing bowl,
   mash the sweet potato into
   a paste. Add the sticky rice
   flour and water and mix
   into a smooth dough.
   Divide the soft dough into
   30~36 pieces the size of a
   cherry.

3. To make the filling: For a richer-tasting bean paste filling, add 1 teaspoon of cinnamon powder or any flavoring of your choice to the red bean paste.

4. To form the sesame balls: On a smooth kitchen table, begin making the sesame balls. Take a dough piece in your hand. First, shape it into a ball, then use your thumb to hollow out the center until it resembles a deep bowl. Drop about 1 teaspoon of bean paste filling in the center of the dough. Carefully pinch the top edges together, then gather the rest of the edges to seal. Use both hands and shape into round balls. Roll the rice balls over the sesame seeds until well coated. Repeat with the rest of filling and dough balls.

5. Heat 2 cups of oil over medium high heat. Test the temperature by sticking a chopstick in the oil. When bubbles appear, it is ready. Deep-fry the sesame balls in small batches until they turn a golden color. Transfer to a deep dish or bowls filled with a small amount of taro sauce and serve immediately. For best results, fry just enough to eat on the same day and refrigerate the rest.

Makes 25 balls

Note

Taro-- This papaya sized native Chinese potato has an intense aroma reminiscent of chestnuts. The wonderful part of this root vegetable is that it tastes great in savory dishes as well as in desserts. You can use it as you would with regular potatoes, but be sure to look for fresh-ness. For this dish, try to find a taro that has moist-looking brown skin since dryness can cause it to lose both taste and texture. A sure sign of freshness is that when you cut it open, you see shiny white flesh speckled with purple streaks.

花生椰子球

Snow Balls with Peanut Butter Filling

Soft rice balls with creamy peanut butter filling (which are sold at Chinese markets) are one of the few Chinese desserts that have found their way to American tables. To give the original recipe a continental appeal, I have changed the peanut butter sesame filling to peanut butter chocolate filling. And I was right in doing so — the response has been wonderful.

Rice Dough
3 1/2 cup sticky rice flour
1 1/2 cup water,
   approximately
1/3 cup sugar
1 cup coconut flakes
orange-colored candied fruit
   for garnish

Peanut Filling
10 Reeses peanut butter cups
1 cup powdered milk
1/3 cup condensed milk

Method
1. To make the dough: Place the rice flour in a mixing bowl and make a well in the center. In a saucepan, combine the water and sugar and heat for 1 minute. Add half of the lukewarm sugar solution to the rice flour, mixing with a spoon. Gradually add the other half of the sugar solution and mix until the dough almost holds together. To make the dough smooth, you need to do a little more work. Take one piece of rice dough the size of a cherry and place in a small bowl. Steam this small rice dough for 5 minutes until soft. Add this cooked dough to the large dough and knead for 2 minutes until it becomes very smooth.

2. To make the filling: Empty the peanut butter cups in a container. Add the powdered milk and condensed milk, mixing thoroughly until smooth.

3. To make the rice balls: First, divide the dough into pieces the size of a ping-pong ball. Then shape each piece into a round ball. Next, hollow out the center and shape it into a bird's nest. Fill the nest with 1/2 tablespoon of filling. Gently push the edge to the center (smear with a little water if needed) and seal well. Roll the dumpling with both palms to make a very round rice ball. Repeat with the rest of the filling and dough.

4. To cook the rice balls: Bring half a pot of water to a rolling boil. Gently add about half of the rice balls to the boiling water. Cover partially and maintain a gentle boil for 5 minutes or until the rice balls float to the top. Remove to cool slightly and then coat each rice ball with coconut flakes. Garnish with the orange-colored candied fruit. Serve at room temperature on the same day. Leftovers may be stored without refrigeration for about 3~4 days. They will harden slightly. To reheat, steam over medium heat for 10 minutes or until softened. Rice dumplings may also be stored in the refrigerator, but warming is also required before serving.

Makes 30 rice balls

紅豆鍋餅

Pan-Fried Red Bean Cake

This is a simplified version of the store-bought crispy bean cake. To modernize this recipe, I have added some Western spices to enrich the red bean filling. As for the dough, you may use any frozen pastry dough to save a few steps and the result would probably be quite close.

2/3 cup black sesame seeds
oil for sautéing

Dough

2 cups all-purpose flour
1/2 of a 3-ounce package
   cream cheese, softened
2/3 cup hot water (not
   boiling)

Filling

2 2/3 cups cooked red beans
sugar to taste (optional)
1 tablespoon mocha coffee
   powder (optional)
1/3 teaspoon cinnamon
   powder

Method

1. To make the dough: Place
   the flour and cream cheese
   in a medium mixing bowl
   and make a well in the
   center. Pour half of the hot
   water into the well and
   start mixing with a large
   spoon. Add the rest of the
   water to the flour, blending
   well to form a soft dough.
   Let rest in a clear plastic
   bag for at least 20
   minutes.

2. To make the filling: Add
   the mocha coffee powder (if
   using) and the cinnamon

powder to the red bean
paste until the flavor is
intense enough for your
taste.

3. To make the cake: Divide
   the dough into 2 portions
   and roll each portion into a
   1-inch sausage. Cut the
   dough into 10 equal pieces
   and flatten them slightly.
   Use a rolling pin and roll
   each piece into a thin
   round, with the center
   slightly thicker. Drop a
   heaping tablespoon of red
   bean filling in the center,
   gather the edges and pinch
   to seal in the center.
   Flatten the cake slightly,
   smear the top with a little
   water and then dip in
   sesame seeds to coat.
   Repeat with the rest of
   dough and filling.

4. Place the bean cakes on a
   cookie sheet and bake at
   275°F for 35 minutes to
   gently cook the dough.
   Then in a large frying pan,
   heat 2 tablespoons of oil
   over medium heat and
   slowly brown both sides of
   the bean cakes until
   crusty. Pan-fry enough

bean cakes for the day and
save the rest in the
refrigerator. Always serve
the cake warm.

Makes 20 cakes

Note

Frozen or canned red
bean can be purchased
from a Chinese food
store. You can also cook
the red bean paste
yourself. To cook the
read bean paste
yourself, buy 1/2 pound
of raw red beans from a
health food store. Place
the red beans in a
stockpot filled with 10
cups water and soak
overnight. Do not drain
the beans. Add 1 cup of
sugar and boil for 2
hours, adding more
water if necessary. The
cooked beans should
resemble a thick
mixture.

GLOSSARY OF INGREDIENTS

Seasonings and Condiments

Chicken Broth 雞湯

Chicken broth is an important and indispensable ingredient in Chinese cooking. Ready-made canned chicken broth is especially helpful for Chinese cooks in a hurry. Besides adding depth and a smooth taste to foods, it is also very nourishing. For beginners who are unfamiliar with the use of various types of Chinese sauces, chicken broth could be a lifesaver. A little chicken broth (a few tablespoonfuls) mixed with 1 to 2 tablespoons of oyster sauce does a wonderful job for a cook in any stir-fried and braised dishes. With just one can of chicken broth and a few ready-to-use ingredients (frozen or canned corn kernels, mushrooms, ham, etc.), you can create a delectable Chinese soup in just minutes.

Chili Bean Paste 辣椒醬

A prime ingredient in Sichuan and Hunan cuisine, this hot bean paste provides instant lift to bland foods and brings dramatic changes to strong-tasting foods (like some seafood and meats). For this reason, chili bean paste is a very popular seasoning in Chinese households. When used in moderation, a good hot sauce can make a noticeable difference in foods and can perhaps bring confidence to a novice cook. Since the quality of chili bean paste varies significantly from brand to brand in Chinese stores, it is important that you select the right kind.

Chinese Mushrooms

香菇

The Chinese call them "aromatic mushrooms." With a rich meaty taste, only a few dried Chinese mushrooms are needed to transform a plain dish into something special. As such, dried mushrooms play a very important role in Chinese vegetarian cooking. They are a wonderful substitute for meat in a great number of dishes. Prices of dried mushrooms vary, depending on their quality. For home cooking, medium-grade mushrooms are acceptable. Before cooking, always soak mushrooms in water until plump. Stems should be removed since they are too tough to be eaten, but do not discard them as they can be used in soups and stocks for added flavor.

Cooking Oil 油

When presented with the question, "What kind of oil should I use?" I usually tell my students that selecting cooking oil is a matter of personal preference. Years ago peanut oil was considered the best kind in China because corn and vegetable oil were not available then. Nowadays most Chinese households use corn oil or canola oil just like what Westerners do. Oil also functions as a lubricant and a protective coating when added to the marinated meat before cooking. This is a Chinese secret for tenderizing stir-fried meat.

Cornstarch 玉米粉

Without cornstarch many Chinese dishes would lose their attractive glaze and smooth taste. Cornstarch is used in cooking for the following reasons:
* To bind the seasonings and ingredients together.
* To prevent the juice from separating from the ingredients, thus maintaining a more appealing look.
* To act as a heat preserver and to add smoothness to the dish.

Cornstarch is commonly used in meat marinade, sauces, heavy soups, and stewed and braised dishes. Avoid using it in quick fried greens or naturally starchy dishes.

Fermented Black Beans
豆鼓

Although they may look like black currants in appearance, this popular Chinese seasoning has a rich aroma that turns many foods into tasty dishes. They are commonly used in steamed seafood (or spareribs) and in stir-fried meats and seafood. Before using, always rinse out the salt. They work best when combined with garlic, chili, or green bell peppers. Fermented black beans will release more flavor when they are cut into finer pieces and then sautéed for a few seconds before adding the main ingredients. For convenience you might want to buy the bottled black bean sauce, but try to get a reliable brand that can provide a taste close to the original one.

Fish Sauce 魚露

As the name implies, this sauce is made from anchovy extract. It has a mild and subtle taste that is perfect for almost any kind of dish. As I could not find an ideal brand of light soy sauce, I have used fish sauce as a substitute for years and those who learn from me are quite happy with the results of this sauce. There are several brands of fish sauce in a Chinese market. My preference is the "Squid Brand".

Five-Spice Powder
五香粉

This is a powdery blend of five different spices: fennel, clove, cinnamon, star anise and Sichuan peppercorn. Rich and distinctive in taste, this powder is a potent spice for masking the gamy taste of meats and fish. It is commonly used in braised or roasted meats, barbecue marinade and certain dumpling fillings. Because of its tendency to overpower, it is seldom added to stir-fried dishes. Always use it in small amounts.

Hoisin Sauce 海鮮醬

Like Sweet Bean Sauce, this tangy mild sweet sauce is a famous dip for Peking duck and Mu Shu pork. It is also an excellent marinade for barbecue dishes and a delectable ingredient for Chinese salad dressing.

Oyster Sauce 蠔油

Made from oyster abstract and wheat, oyster sauce is the epitome of a classic Chinese idea — using seafood as a flavor enhancer. With more depth and richness than soy sauce, oyster sauce is an effective seasoning for stir-fried and braised dishes, particularly for those on the light side. You can rely on oyster sauce to add life to many simple and bland-tasting vegetables. Oyster sauce doubles the strength of flavoring when combined with chicken broth in stewing dishes. It can also be used along with soy sauce in many ways.

Red Bean Paste 紅豆沙

Creamy, smooth and mildly sweet, red bean paste (which comes in cans or frozen packages) has been the number one filling for many traditional Chinese pastries. Its position in the Chinese pastry kitchen is almost parallel to that of chocolate in Western cuisine. When compared with the rich taste of American desserts, red bean paste might seem a little bland in taste, but this can be easily improved by adding a variety of popular spices, such as vanilla, cinnamon or coconut. Try using it as a spread or mixing it into your sweet sauces. You'll love the smooth taste.

Sesame Oil 麻油

Made from toasted sesame seeds, this brownish oil has a concentrated aroma that is ideal for flavoring foods. Because of its low smoking point and overpowering nature, sesame oil is not recommended as cooking oil. As a basic seasoning ingredient, sesame oil can bring good results in the following areas:
* Use in marinade for meats and seafood as a flavor

enhancer and lubricant.
* Mix in salads for added aroma.
* Brush on roast meats to add a nice glaze.
* Use as a "final touch" to heighten the flavor of soups and stir-fried dishes toward the end of cooking (or the flavor evaporates).

Sha Cha Sauce

(Fire Pot Sauce) 沙茶醬
This wonderful southern-style sauce has been overlooked by many Chinese cookbooks, probably because of its misleading translation. My favorite brand in the market is called the "Bull's Head," but it has been sold under the name of "barbecue sauce" for years. This seems to confuse Western buyers. Every Chinese person knows that sha cha sauce is the best fire pot sauce, but the majority of people are still unaware that sha cha sauce is an all-purpose sauce. This fragrant sauce comes in a small glass or tin jar and is sold only at Chinese markets. Also known as sha cha sauce.

Sichuan Peppercorns
花椒
Sharp and powerful, these tiny brown peppercorns are totally different from their Western counterpart. Because of their effective odor-suppressing property,

Sichuan peppercorns are used in all regions of China for marinating meats and poultry. Peppercorn oil, which is made by immersing peppercorn in hot oil (peppercorns are discarded after the flavor is extracted), has a strong aroma that can uplift the taste of any food dramatically. Sichuan peppercorns come in plastic bags and are available at most Chinese markets.

Sichuan Pickled Mustard Green 榨菜
Spicy and flavorful, this Sichuan relish is an important seasoning and garnish for many home-style dishes. This product comes in cans or plastic bags, in either whole or shredded form. To use this preserved vegetable properly, follow these guidelines:
* Rinse out the spice and salt if you like it lighter.
* Use in hot and sour soup or other clear soup for added flavor and texture.
* Chop finely and use in cold noodles and salads.
* Store the unused pickled mustard green in the refrigerator; it will keep for months.

Soy Sauce 醬油
There is no doubt about the versatility of soy sauce—the question lies in how to choose

the right brand and how to use it properly. Do not be misled by the impression that Chinese food should be darkened in soy sauce. Except in stewing and roasting meat dishes, soy sauce should be used in moderation to bring out the best results in taste and color. Here are some helpful guidelines:
* Buy medium-grade soy sauce so that it can be used either in dishes that need heavy coloring (use more) or in those that require light touches (simply use a smaller quantity).
* When used as a marinade, soy sauce should be blended with other ingredients such as wine, sugar, spices, ginger, garlic, or scallions for best results.
* Soy sauce adds saltiness to food; thus, one should use it with restraint. When using soy sauce, decrease or completely omit the amount of added salt to avoid excessive saltiness.
* When eating in a Chinese restaurant, do not add soy sauce to food before tasting since most Chinese dishes are fully seasoned. In many cases, saltiness can ruin the taste of the food.

Star Anise 八角
Possessing a strong aroma, this star-shaped spice is the most important of the five

spices. It is widely used in braised, stewed and cold-cut dishes. Because of its overpowering character, star anise should be used sparingly; add only one or two stars to a dish. It keeps indefinitely in a cool, dry place.

Sugar and Rock Sugar
糖、冰糖

Sugar has a distinct place in Chinese cooking. Its function is not to sweeten but to smooth up the taste when a dish is too flat or a little salty. Mixing in a small amount of sugar can correct the situation. Rock sugar is a light-brown or amber-colored crystal. It is commonly used in desserts or stewing meat dishes. Apart from lending a delicate taste, rock sugar adds an attractive glaze to meats. It is sold in plastic bags or paper boxes in Chinese stores.

Vinegar 醋

Vinegar is an essential seasoning ingredient in many Chinese dishes. Although most Chinese do not care for sweet and sour dishes adapted to Western tastes, They do like lightly seasoned sweet-and-sour dishes prepared by experienced cooks.

Chinese use vinegar in:
* Sweet-and-sour sauces for stir-fried dishes.
* Pickling or marinating juices for vegetable salads.
* Dipping sauces for dim sums and fried foods.
* Hot-and-sour soups or stir-fried dishes.
Here are some tips on choosing the right vinegar to match your dishes although you may vary your choice according to your personal taste:
* Cider vinegar, white vinegar or rice vinegar for pickled or sweet-and-sour dishes if you want to retain the natural colors of your vegetable dishes.
* Balsamic vinegar or red wine vinegar in dipping sauces or hot-and-sour soups for a richer taste.
* Chinese dark vinegar is usually infused with vegetable juices and spices which imparts a stronger flavor than balsamic vinegar. You may want to try it in dipping sauces and soups as you would balsamic vinegar.

Wine 酒

Wine is an indispensable ingredient in almost any kind of good cooking. One of the secrets in Chinese cooking is in the proper use of wine. The Chinese use wine in marinades to eliminate the gamy taste of meats and the fishy smell of seafood and to help bring out their rich taste. Even in certain vegetable dishes, a sprinkle of wine can bring unexpected good results. Choose a cooking wine that has a light but deep flavor such as rice wine or dry sherry. Shaoxing (Shao Hsing) rice wine, which is available in most Chinese food stores, is highly regarded by most Chinese cooks as the best cooking wine for meats.

Wood Ears (Tree Ears)
木耳

These belong to the black mushroom family. The Chinese call them "wood-ears." Wood ears have no flavor of their own. They are used in stir-fried dishes and soups mainly to add color and texture. According to Chinese classic cookbooks, wood ears are good for the heart. This might interest the health conscious. Like dried Chinese mushrooms, wood ears need to be soaked a few minutes before cooking. They usually expand to three times their size, so use only a small amount each time you cook.

Vegetables

Baby Bok Choy 青江菜
Beautifully shaped like a miniature tree, this cabbage, which is also called Shanghai bok choy, is often used as a decorative vegetable for many elegant banquet dishes. Unlike the regular bok choy, baby bok choy has spoon-shaped stems of pale green color. It is stronger in taste than napa cabbage but is just as sweet and tasty when stir-fried and braised.

Bamboo Shoots 竹筍
Bamboo shoots are considered a delicacy—the caviar of vegetables. Unfortunately, to this day, no one has ever been able to produce fresh bamboo shoots on this continent. The newly imported frozen "Green Bamboo Shoots" (this is the brand name: they are actually off-white) come very close to the fresh ones in China. Your next choice would be the canned "Green Bamboo Shoots." Quality bamboo shoots are excellent ingredients for stir-fried dishes, soups and salads. If good bamboo shoots are unavailable, substitute crisp fresh vegetables such as cucumber, celery or asparagus.

Bean Sprouts 豆芽
Bean sprouts are excellent for stir-fried dishes and salads. But insist on freshness. Do not buy yellowed and wilted sprouts; look for the plump and shiny white ones. The best bean sprouts are usually sold at Chinese vegetable stands in Chinatown and some Oriental markets. Bean sprouts have a crisp texture but a very bland taste. For better results, cook with shredded meats or aromatic vegetables, such as onions, scallions, or green bell peppers. Some home cooks consider Chinese chives or basil the best accompaniments to bean sprouts in a meatless dish. When used in salad dishes, bean sprouts should be boiled briefly to eliminate the muddy taste.

Chinese Eggplants
中國茄子
Long and slender in shape and bright purple in color, Chinese eggplants are an attractive member of the eggplant family. Unlike other members of the eggplant family, Chinese eggplants have a finer flesh with a delicate taste. Use them the same way as you would in your familiar eggplant recipes but you don't need to salt them since the Chinese eggplants are not bitter but have a natural sweetness.

Cilantro (Coriander)
芫茜（香菜）
This Chinese parsley is an effective flavor enhancer in many dishes. Like scallions, it adds taste to soups, salads, braised dishes and dumpling fillings without overpowering them. Cilantro looks pretty in color and in shape, which makes it a ready garnish for a great number of dishes. Cilantro is sold in bundles in Chinese food markets and some supermarkets. It keeps up to ten days in the refrigerator if well wrapped in plastic bags.

Daikon 蘿蔔
(Chinese Radish)
The Chinese radish is known as daikon to people in this country. Like the American radish, the Chinese radish is pungent and sharp, but it becomes juicy and slightly sweet once cooked. It is used extensively in relishes, salads and stewed dishes; it also makes a tasty filling in a number of dumplings and pastries (the Chinese radish cake, also known as Chinese turnip cake, is a favorite of Chinese dim sum diners). It is now available in some supermarkets and all Asian stores. When buying daikon, avoid the dried, fibrous roots; select the heavier ones with shiny white skin. Daikon, like napa cabbage, has a high water content and must be

drained thoroughly before use in stir-fried and salad dishes.

Garlic 大蒜

Like the French and Italians, the Chinese use garlic as a prime seasoning to add depth and aroma to a great number of dishes. In stir-fried, salad, seafood and pickled dishes, garlic is an indispensable ingredient. In many cases, it outweighs ginger in importance. Although there are new devices to crush the garlic and remove the skin, Chinese cooks prefer to do this with the heavy blade of a cleaver on a cutting board.

Ginger 薑

The West has finally discovered the potency of ginger. Its pungent sharp taste provides a powerful suppressant for fishy or gamy odors. For this reason, it is indispensable when cooking fish and meat dishes. Besides being used extensively in stir-fried and stewed meat dishes, a small amount of minced ginger is often added to meatballs and dumplings with excellent results. Ginger is also a very useful herb in Chinese folk medicine. Ginger and brown sugar soup is often used in Chinese households to combat minor colds.

Napa Cabbage 山東白菜

This Chinese cabbage is extremely versatile. It blends well with any flavor and fits into almost any form of cooking. In Chinese home cooking, napa cabbage is the choice ingredient for stir-fried, braised and pickled dishes, and in soups. It is also the most popular vegetable for meat dumplings. The addition of cabbage makes the filling of egg rolls and pork buns lighter in taste and texture. Another advantage of using this cabbage is the convenience. Napa cabbage cooks in three minutes and it even keeps for days without refrigeration if wrapped in paper.

Scallions and Onions 蔥、洋蔥

Ginger, scallions and garlic, the three basic seasoning aromatics, play an extremely important role in Chinese cuisine. They are used separately in most stir-fried dishes; however, dishes with a strong taste usually call for all three. Scallions, with their mild taste and pleasing aroma, seem to top all the seasoning herbs in versatility. Almost any dish can taste better with a spoonful of chopped scallions. Here are some tips on using scallions efficiently:

* Mixing in scallions (chopped) with marinated meats can mask unpleasant tastes.
* Sautéing the scallion stem (white portion) in oil creates a nice aroma for stir-fried dishes
* Adding minced scallions to dumpling filling enhances the flavor.
* Garnishing soups with scallions adds color and taste.

When scallions are in short supply, which often occurs, onions are an excellent substitute for sautéing. Although onions are less fragrant, they are easier to obtain and to store.

Taro 大芋頭

This is an intriguing root vegetable available only at the Chinese markets. Oval in shape with rough brown skin, the taro root is the size of a papaya and tastes like chestnuts. It may be best described as "the Chinese potato" as both the potato and taro are very starchy. It is an unusual vegetable that can be used in main dishes as well as in a few astonishingly tasty desserts. Taro may look a little too exotic for Westerners, but it has many virtues waiting to be discovered by the adventurous cook.

Rice and Noodles

Rice 米

Many of my students ask which type of rice is better— long-grain or short-grain. There is no definite answer since this is strictly a matter of personal preference. Although most Chinese restaurants use long-grain rice owing to its popularity with Western diners, many Chinese households are partial to short-grain rice for its resilient texture and deeper flavor. According to the experienced home cook, the best-tasting rice is made by blending the two kinds of rice together at a ratio of one to one.

Brown Rice 糙米

This is higher in fiber and natural nutrients than regular white rice. Although many people use brown rice for health reasons, few people know how to prepare it properly. To produce the best-tasting brown rice, you need to blend it with white rice at a ratio of one to one or to your personal taste. Since brown rice takes longer to cook, it is necessary to soak it for at least 1 hour before cooking. When it has expanded slightly, mix in white rice, add water to cover about 3/4 of an inch above the rice and steam for 35 to 40 minutes. The end result is a pot of fluffy and flavorful light brown rice.

Sticky Rice (Sweet Rice or Glutinous Rice) 糯米

This favorite rice product of the Orient is still a novelty to most Westerners. Only those who have tasted the mouth-watering dim sum or other sweets made from sweet rice know how marvelous it can be. The resilient and sticky texture, the result of its high starch content, is the distinctive characteristic of sticky rice. For this reason, it is not suitable for daily consumption. Sweet rice is the staple of festival foods and numerous delectable savories and sweets are made from it.

Chinese Noodles 中國粉麵

Western pasta fans will find it worth their effort to explore the rich varieties of Chinese noodles. Besides expanding your repertoire of pastas, these products will probably save you some money on your purchase. Many Chinese noodles have excellent texture and taste, yet cost much less than the Western gourmet noodles sold in supermarkets and specialty food stores. Chinese noodles may be roughly divided into two categories— wheat noodles and rice noodles.

Wheat Noodles 麵條

There are two types of wheat noodles in the market:

Refrigerated fresh noodles: 濕麵條
Both Shanghai noodles and Cantonese noodles are packed fresh in plastic bags. The Shanghai noodles are more elastic, which seems to please people from all regions. These cook in 4 to 7 minutes, depending on the brand. Those who like noodles with a softer texture prefer the Cantonese egg noodles, which taste strongly of eggs. You need to use special care in cooking these noodles. They tend to stick together if overcooked. Cook them in boiling water for about 2 minutes.

Dried noodles: 乾麵條
These usually occupy a large portion of the shelf in the store. It is almost impossible to try every kind. The one-

pound white thin noodles in plastic bags from Taiwan are generally good.

For a bowl of well-cooked noodles, you need to follow these rules:
* Always bring the water to a vigorous boil before adding the noodles.
* Cook a small amount of noodles in a large amount of water. The water should be at least triple the quantity of noodles to allow for expansion.
* The ideal consistency of the cooked noodles should be soft but still elastic.

Rice Noodles 粉類

There are many types of rice noodles but there is one type which is used widely—rice sticks. Rice sticks look like transparent angel hair, but in their dried form are as hard as steel wires. They need to be soaked in water for a few minutes in order to be cut into shorter lengths. Cook the rice sticks in chicken broth for about 3 to 4 minutes, then garnish with soy sauce, sesame oil, cilantro and shredded meats or meat sauce. They are resilient, slippery and taste marvelous.

Cellophane Noodles
粉絲

Cellophane noodles are a remarkable product. They are healthy, tasty, versatile, inexpensive and very easy to cook. These are not considered a regular noodle since they are made from mung bean starch. Cellophane noodles may be bland by themselves, but they can soak up flavor quickly during cooking and become bouncy and tasty. They are ideal in stir-fried dishes, soups, salads and vegetarian dishes. Before using, cellophane noodles need to be soaked in water until softened, then cut into convenient lengths. It is important not to overcook them. It is equally important to select a good brand, such as Lung Kow, which endures heat a little longer.

Spring Roll Wrappers and Wonton Wrappers
春卷皮、餛飩皮

Did you know that Spring Rolls are different from the popular "Egg Rolls" you buy from take-out restaurants? Egg rolls are made with wrappers of egg dough, which yield thicker and less crisp rolls, whereas spring rolls are made with thinner flour wrappers and delicately flavored fillings that yield tastier rolls. Spring rolls are refined versions of the popular egg rolls and are sold at better Chinese restaurants.

Personally, I find making spring roll wrappers and wonton wrappers uneconomical, since the procedure is labor-intensive and commercial wrappers cost so little. On the supermarket shelf, egg roll wrappers and wonton wrappers are almost identical in terms of thickness and shape. The large squares are for wrapping egg rolls and the small squares are for wontons. Spring roll wrappers are available only at Chinese food markets. For your own convenience, the next time you visit a Chinese food market, purchase more than one package and store in your freezer, as they keep many months without changing texture.

Index